HISTORY
OF THE
WAR IN SOUTH AFRICA
1899–1902

COMPILED BY DIRECTION OF
HIS MAJESTY'S GOVERNMENT

BY

MAJOR-GENERAL SIR FREDERICK MAURICE, K.C.B.

WITH A STAFF OF OFFICERS

MAPS • VOLUME II

The Naval & Military Press Ltd

Published by
The Naval & Military Press Ltd
5 Riverside, Brambleside, Bellbrook
Industrial Estate, Uckfield, East Sussex,
TN22 1QQ England
Tel: +44 (0) 1825 749494
Fax: +44 (0) 1825 765701
www.naval-military-press.com

In reprinting in facsimile from the original, any imperfections are inevitably reproduced and the quality may fall short of modern type and cartographic standards.

LIST OF MAPS AND FREEHAND SKETCHES.
VOL. II.

MAPS.

No. 18.	Operations on the Upper Tugela.	January 10th to February 10th, 1900.	
No. 19.	Spion Kop.	January 17th to 26th, 1900.	*Area of Operations.*
No. 19 (A).	Spion Kop.	January 17th, 1900.	*Position of Troops at Sunset.*
No. 19 (B).	Spion Kop.	January 18th, 1900.	*Position of Troops at Sunset.*
No. 19 (C).	Spion Kop.	January 19th, 1900.	*Position of Troops at Sunset.*
No. 19 (D).	Spion Kop.	January 20th, 1900.	*Position of Troops at Sunset.*
No. 19 (E).	Spion Kop.	January 21st, 1900.	*Position of Troops at Sunset.*
No. 19 (F).	Spion Kop.	January 22nd, 1900.	*Position of Troops at Sunset.*
No. 19 (G).	Spion Kop.	January 23rd, 1900.	*Position of Troops at Sunset.*
No. 19 (H).	Spion Kop.	January 24th, 1900.	*Position of Troops at Sunset.*
No. 19 (I).	Spion Kop.	January 25th, 1900.	*Position of Troops at Sunset.*
No. 19 (J).	Spion Kop.	January 26th, 1900.	*Position of Troops at Sunset.*
No. 20.	Spion Kop.	January 24th, 1900.	*The Situation at about 9 a.m.*
No. 20 (A).	Spion Kop.	January 24th, 1900.	*The Situation at about 3 p.m.*
No. 20 (B.)	Spion Kop.	January 24th, 1900.	*The Situation at Sunset.*
No. 21.	Vaal Krantz.	February 5th, 1900.	*Position of Troops at 11 a.m.*
No. 21 (A).	Vaal Krantz.	February 5th, 1900.	*Position of Troops at Sunset.*
No. 21 (B).	Vaal Krantz.	February 6th, 1900.	*Position of Troops at Midnight.*
No. 21 (C).	Vaal Krantz.	February 7th, 1900.	*Position of Troops at Sunset.*
No. 22.	Relief of Kimberley.	February 10th—14th, 1900.	*Movements of Troops.*
No. 22 (A).	Relief of Kimberley.	February 15th, 1900.	*Movements of Troops.*
No. 22 (B).	Relief of Kimberley.	February 16th and 17th, 1900.	*Movements of Troops.*
No. 23.	Paardeberg.	February 18th, 1900.	*Situation about 8 a.m.*
No. 23 (A.)	Paardeberg.	February 18th—19th, 1900.	*Situation at Night.*
No. 24.	Protected Bivouac and Works near Paardeberg.	February 21st to 27th, 1900.	
No. 25.	Paardeberg to Bloemfontein.	February—March, 1900.	
No. 26.	Poplar Grove.		
No. 27.	Driefontein.	*Situation at 3.30 p.m.*	
No. 28.	Environs of Kimberley.	*Situation early in February*, 1900.	
No. 29.	Kimberley.	*British Works and Positions at the End of the Siege.*	
No. 30.	Relief of Ladysmith.	February 17th to 27th, 1900.	*Area of Operations.*
No. 30 (A).	Relief of Ladysmith.	February 18th, 1900.	
No. 30 (B).	Relief of Ladysmith.	February 22nd, 1900.	
No. 30 (C).	Relief of Ladysmith.	February 23rd, 1900.	
No. 30 (D).	Relief of Ladysmith.	February 27th, 1900.	
No. 31.	Defence of Ladysmith.		
No. 32.	Ladysmith.	January 6th, 1900.	Action at Wagon Hill and Cæsar's Camp. *Situation at 2 p.m.*
No. 32 (A).	Ladysmith.	January 6th, 1900.	Action at Wagon Hill and Cæsar's Camp. *Situation at 5 p.m.*
No. 33.	Sannah's Post.		
No. 34.	Wepener.		
No. 35.	North-West of Cape Colony.	March, April and May, 1900.	*Area of Operations.*
No. 36.	South Africa.	Map showing the approximate situation on the 1st May, 1900.	
No. 37.	Index Map to Volume II.		

FREEHAND SKETCHES.

Upper Tugela.	Relief of Ladysmith. *View from Clump Hill.*
Potgieters Drift.	Relief of Ladysmith. *View from Hart's Hill.*
Colesberg.	Ladysmith.

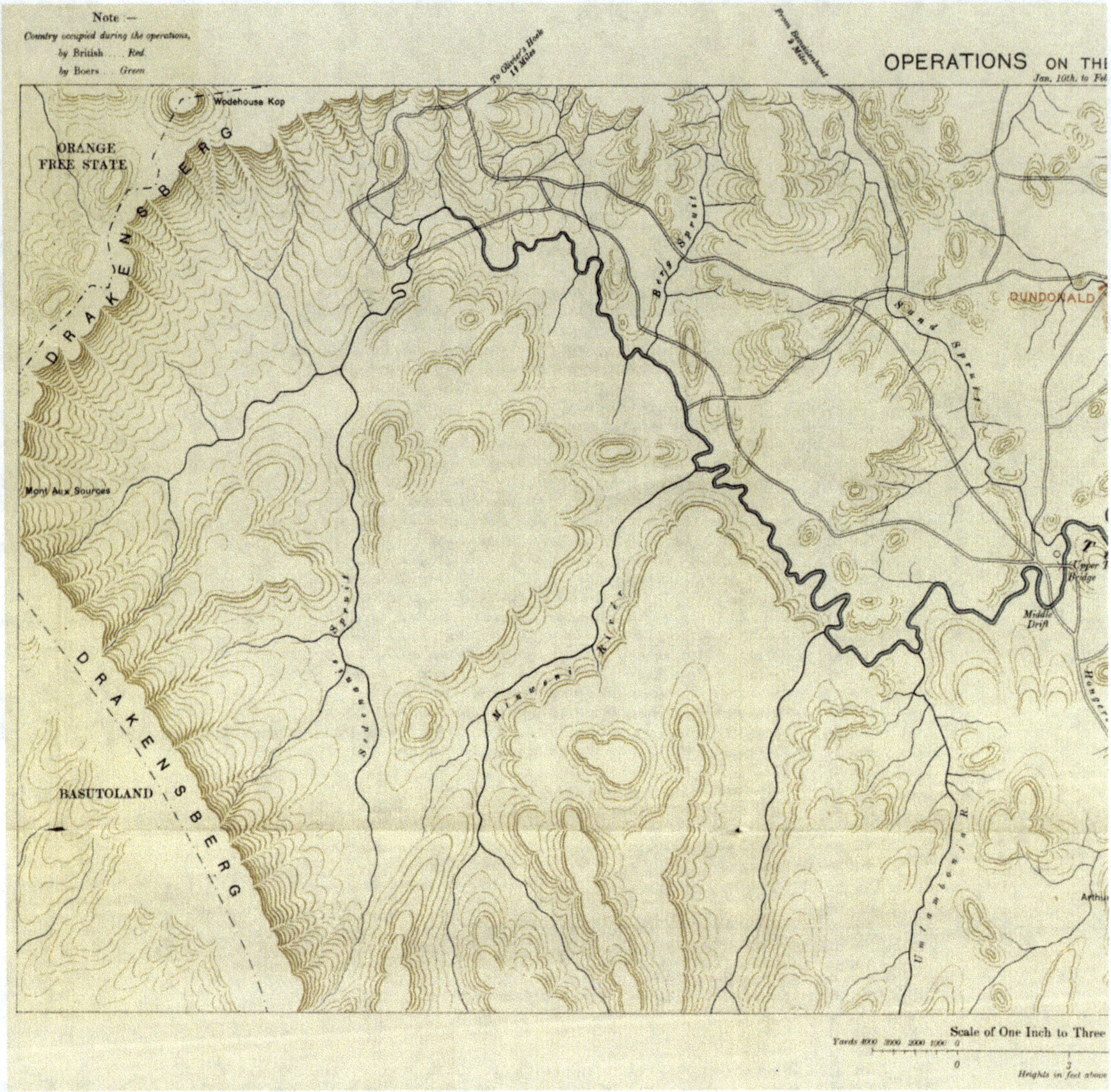

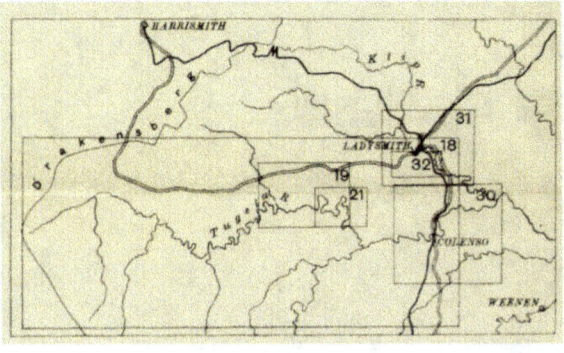

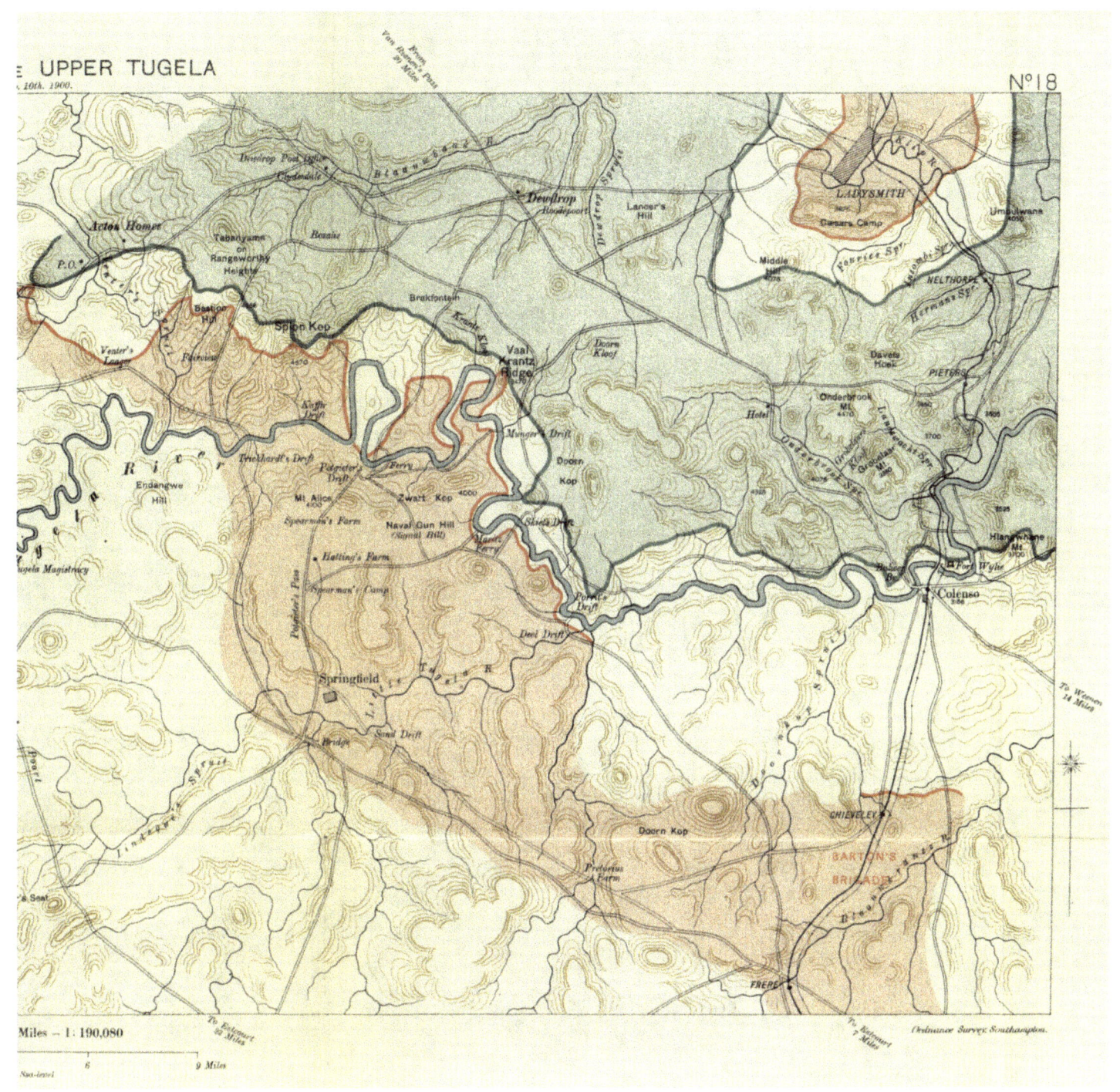

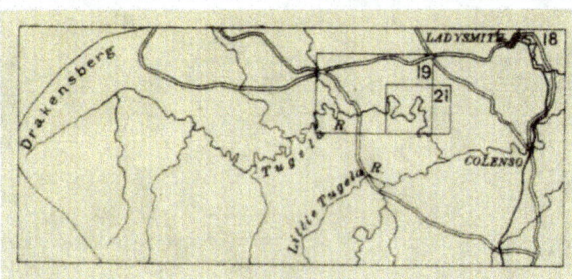

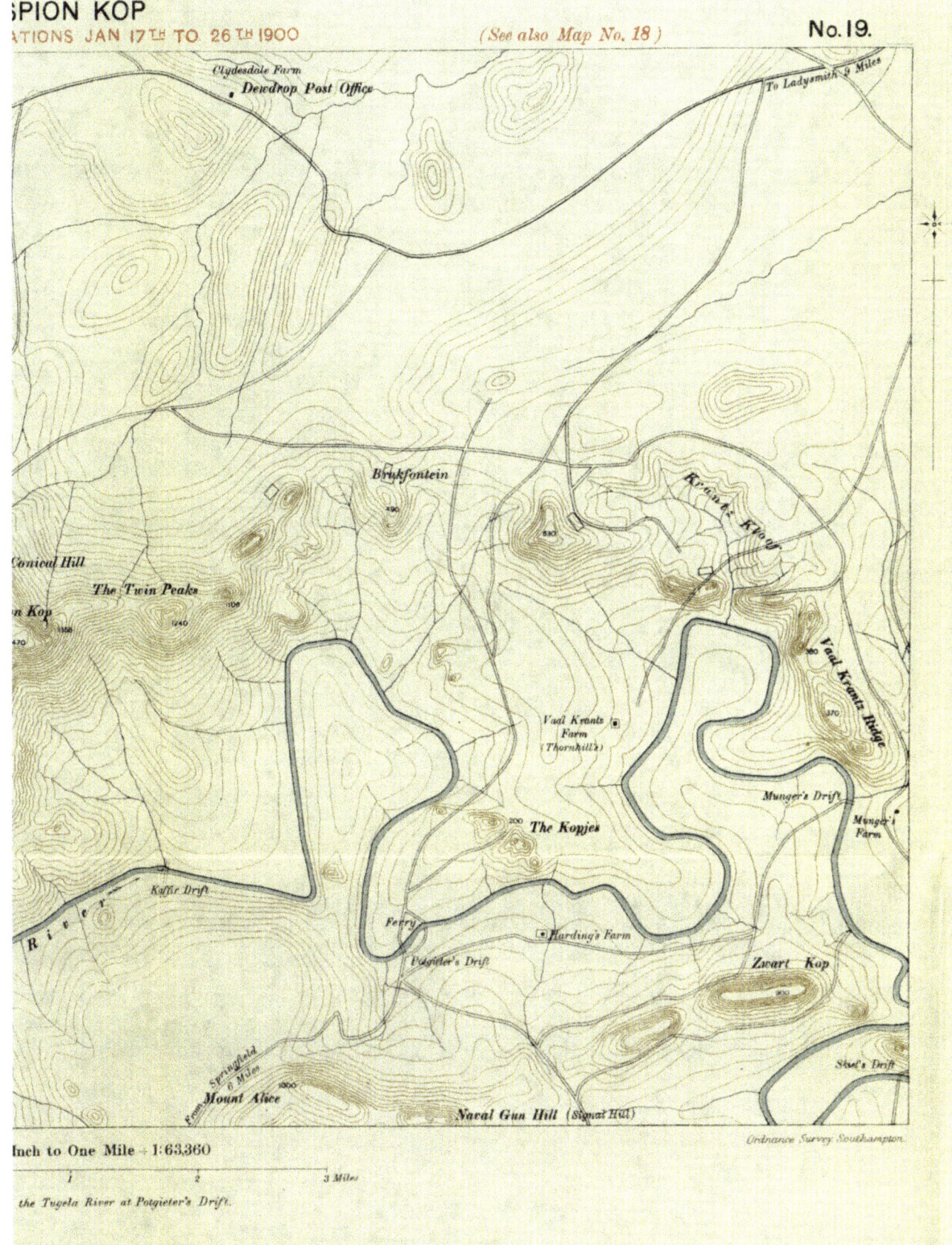

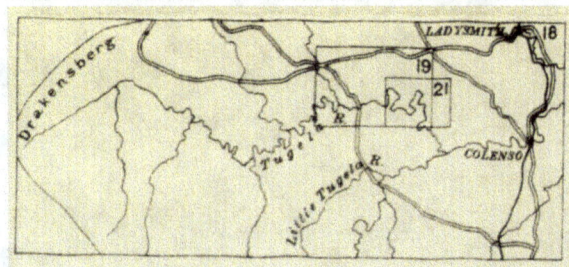

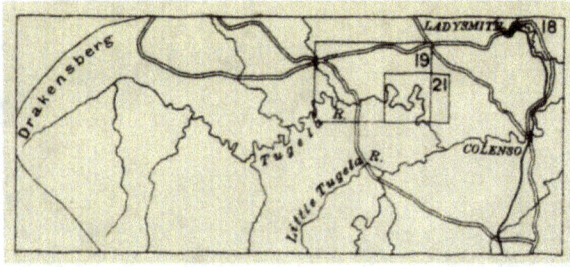

S
POSITION OF TROOP
BOER GUN
Acton Homes
BOER GUN
Acton Homes Farm
Frere Store
1142
LAAGER
Rangeworthy Heights
(Tabanyama)
GENERAL LOUIS BOTHA
Sol de Jager
Long Kopje
Rosalie
From Olivier's Hoek, 24 Miles
From Venter's Laager Road Junction, 5 Miles
To Advanced Post Mounted Brigade, 2 Miles
Venter's Spruit
Bastion Hill
Three Tree Hill
Green Hill
Piquet Hill
DUNDONALD'S HEADQUARTERS
Earthcote
ROYAL DNS
Fairview
LAN. FUS.
YORK & LANC.
DEVON (3 COS.)
Venter's Laager
19 & 28 R.F.A.
63 R.F.A.
Farm
R. LANC.
7 R.F.A.
S. LAN.
T. M. I.
From Acton Homes Road Junction, 3¼ Miles
DEVON (5 COS.)
QUEENS
Venter's Spruit Drift
R.E.
W. YORK.
CONN. RANG.
R. INNIS. FUS.
BORDER
Trestle Bridge
R. DUB. FUS.
E. SURR.
73 & 78 R.F.A.
Wright's Farm
Trickhardt's Drift
Tugela
SOM. L. I. (2 COS.)
Trickhardt's Farm
Pontoon Bridge
To Frere
Scale of One
Yards 2000 1500 1000 500 0
0
Heights in Feet above

Drakensberg
LADYSMITH
18
19
21
Tugela R.
Little Tugela R.
COLENSO

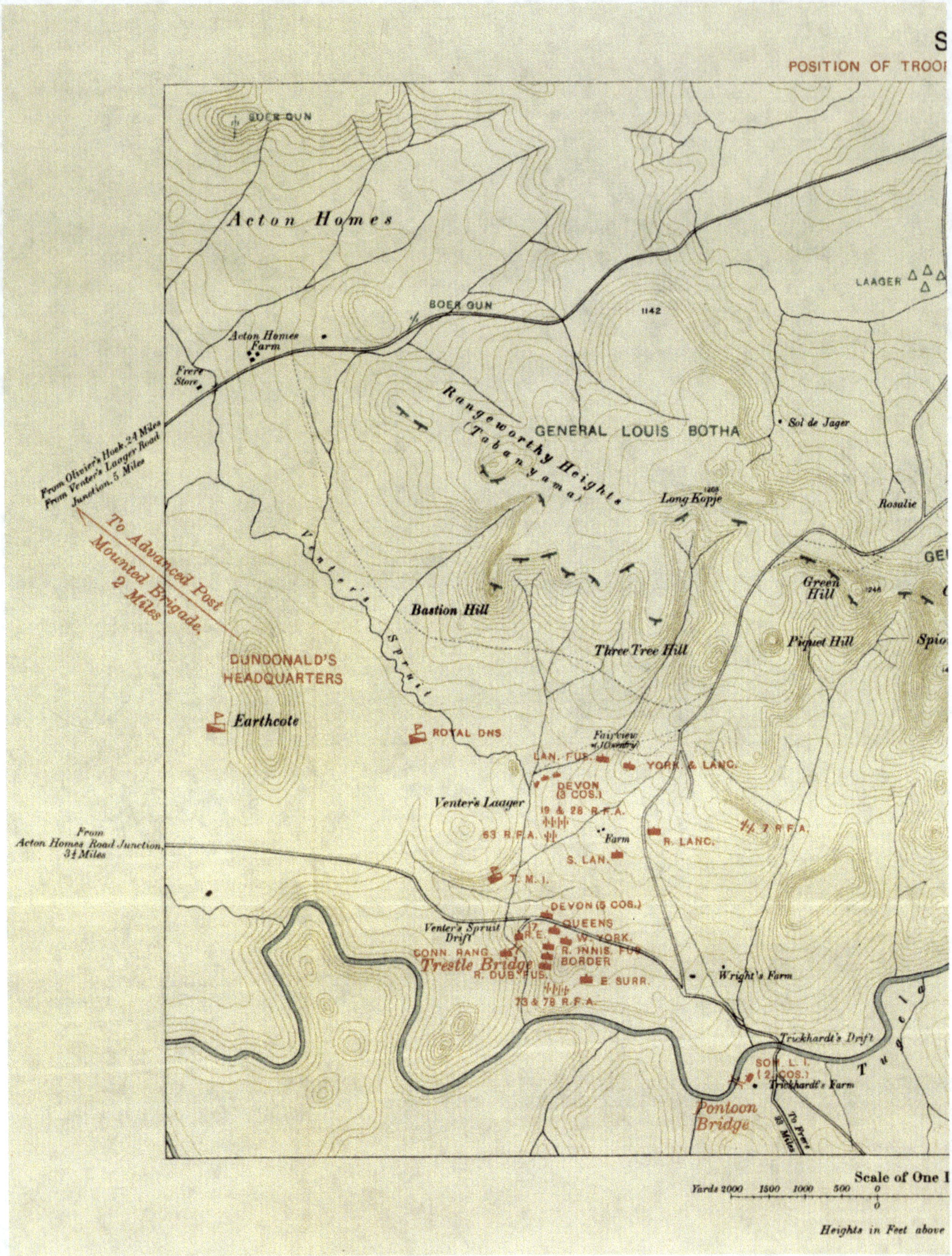

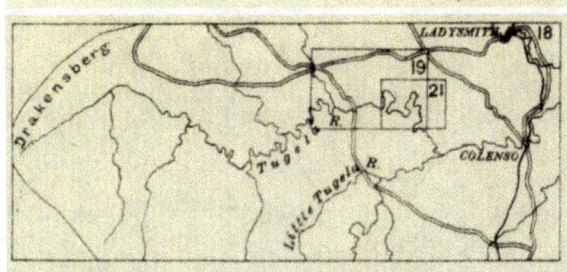

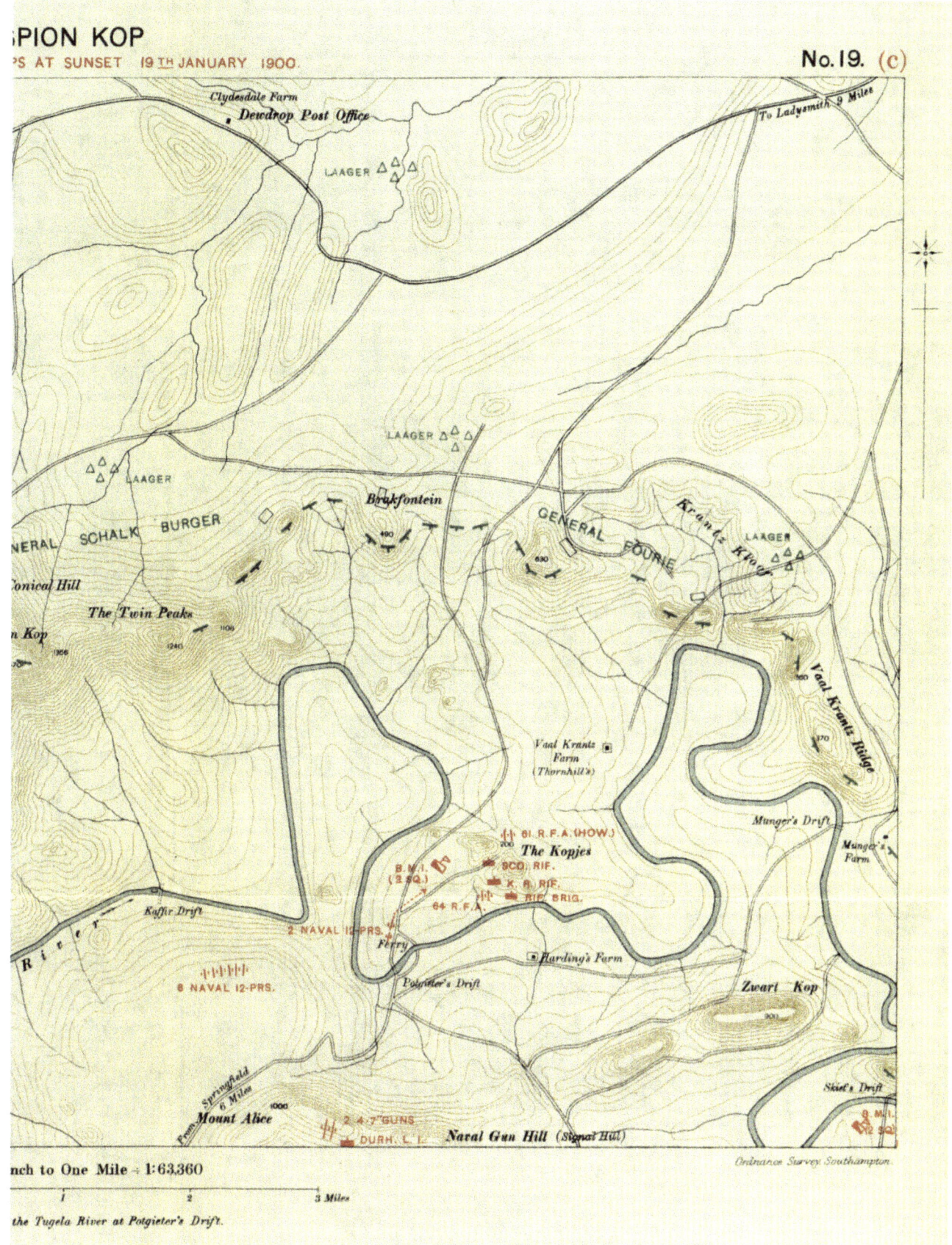

POSITION OF TROOP
BOER GUN
Acton Homes
LAAGER
BOER GUN
1142
Acton Homes Farm
Frere Store
Rangeworthy Heights
(Tabanyama)
GENERAL LOUIS BOTHA
Sol de Jager
From Olivier's Hoek 24 Miles
From Venter's Laager Road Junction, 5 Miles
Long Kopje
2 BOER GUNS
Rosalie
To Advanced Post Mounted Brigade, 2 Miles
Venter's Spruit
E. SURR.
DEVON
YORK & LANC.
LAN. FUS.
BORDER
R. DUB. FUS.
R. INNIS. FUS. (5 COS.)
Green Hill
Bastion Hill
R. INNIS. FUS. (3 COS.)
S. LAN. (2 COS.)
W. YORK
Three Tree Hill
Piquet Hill
DUNDONALD'S HEADQUARTERS
ROYAL DNS.
R. LANC.
S. LAN. (6 COS.)
CONN. RANG.
Earthcote
LAN. FUS. (PIQUETS)
17 R.E.
CONN. RANG.
Fairview
R.F.A.
QUEENS
Venter's Laager
From Acton Homes Road Junction, 3¼ Miles
Farm
Venter's Spruit Drift
T.M.I.
Wright's Farm
Trickhardt's Drift
Tugela
SOM. L.I. (2 COS.)
Trickhardt's Farm
Pontoon Bridge
To Frere 18 Miles
Scale of One
Yards 2000 1500 1000 500 0
Heights in Feet above

Drakensberg
LADYSMITH
18
19
21
Tugela R.
COLENSO
Little Tugela R.

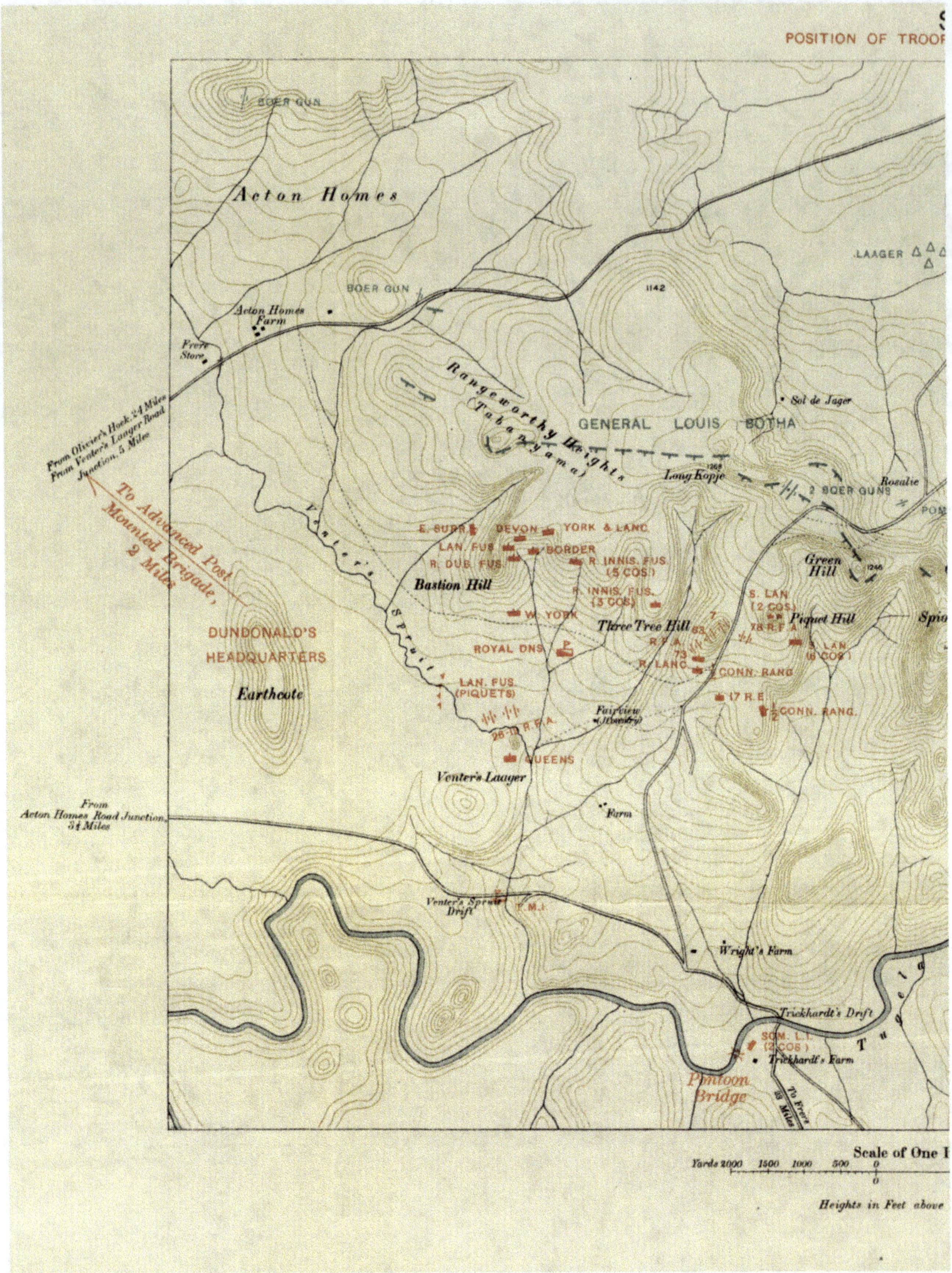

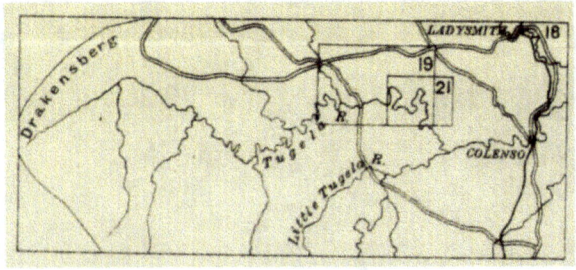

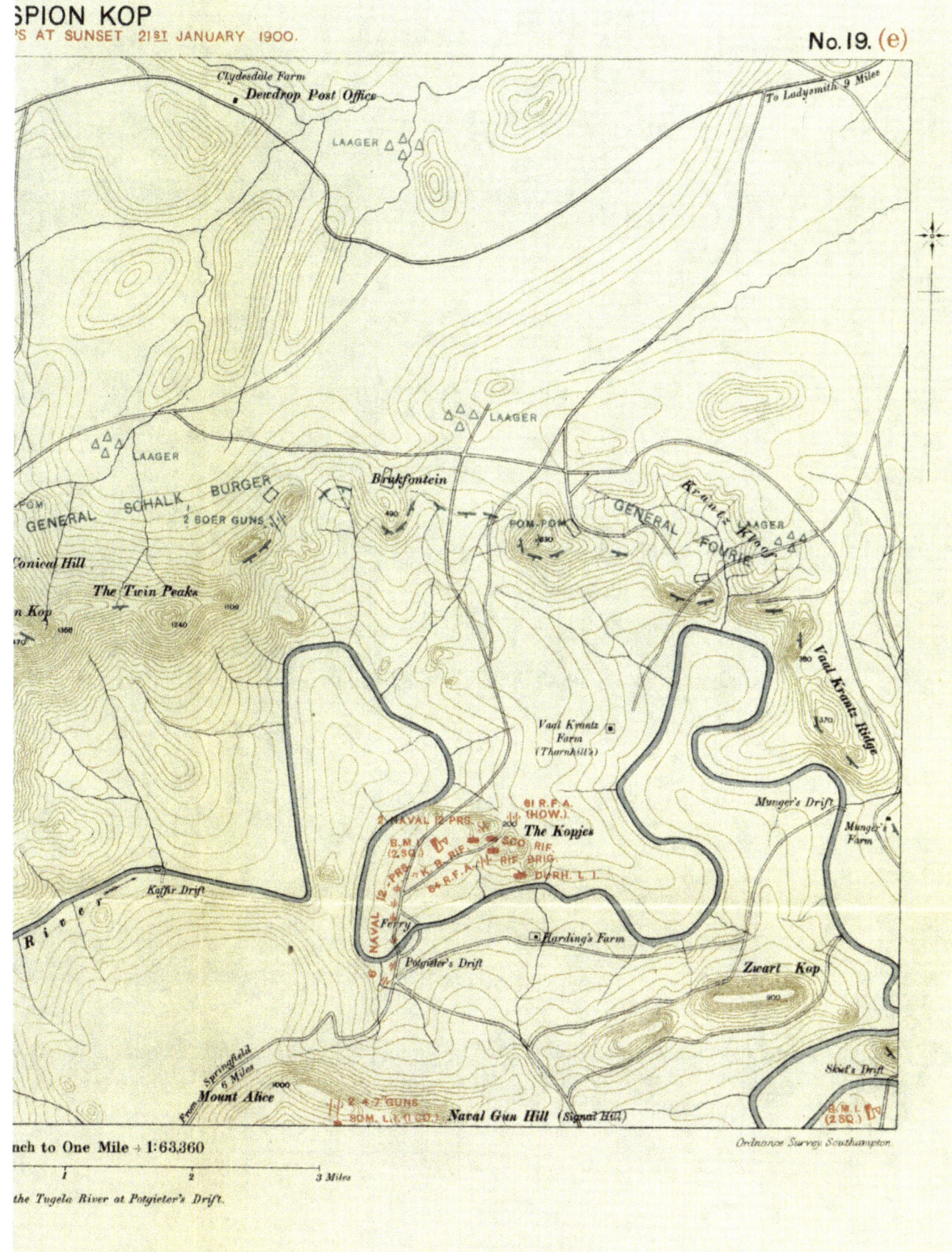

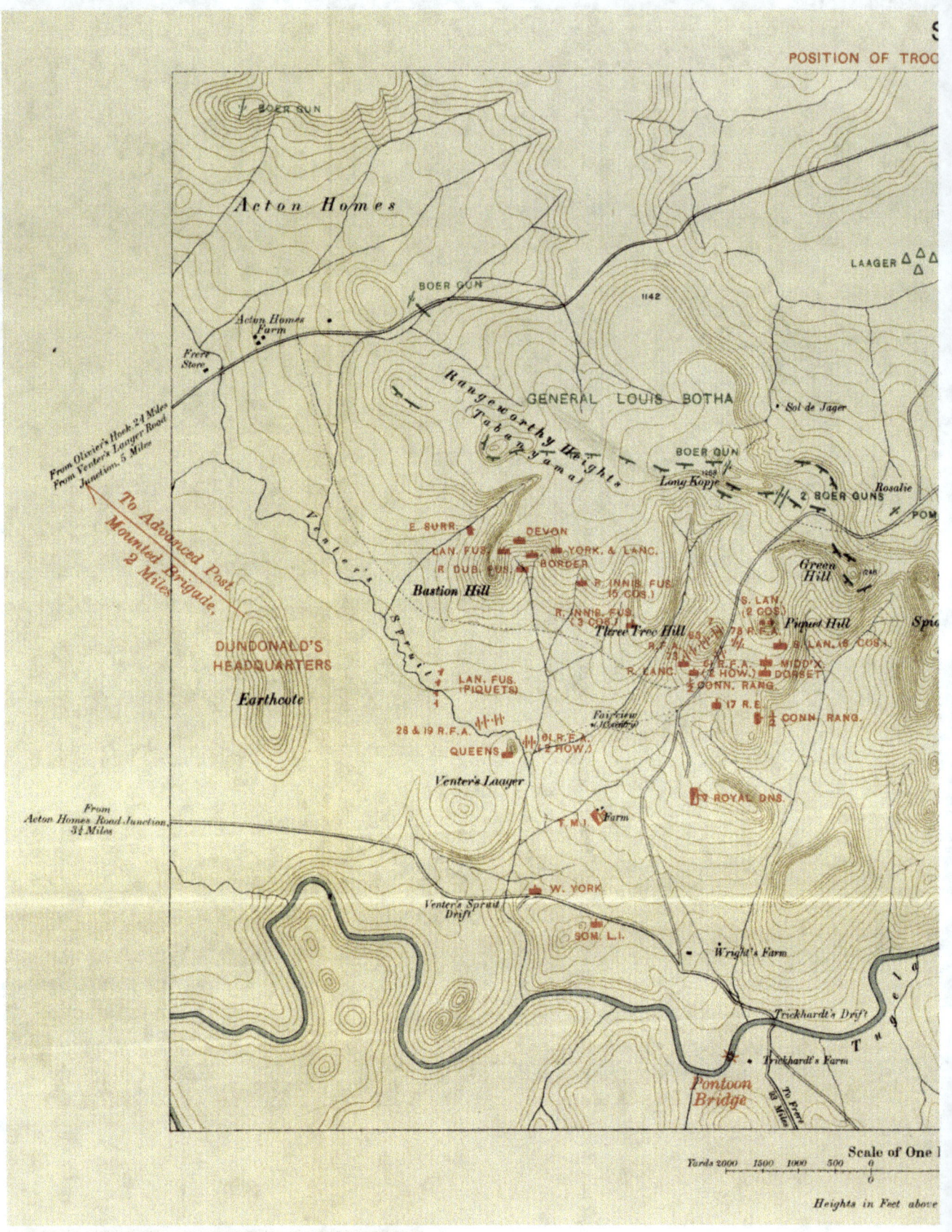

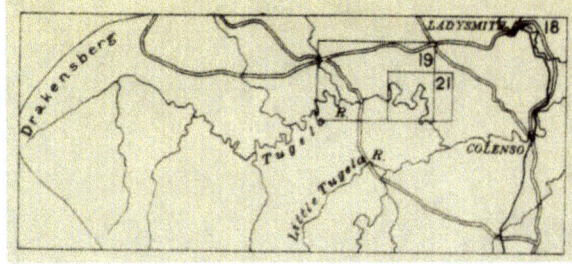

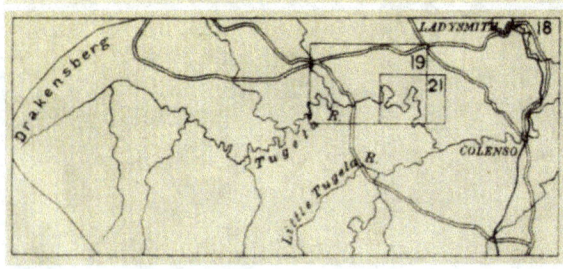

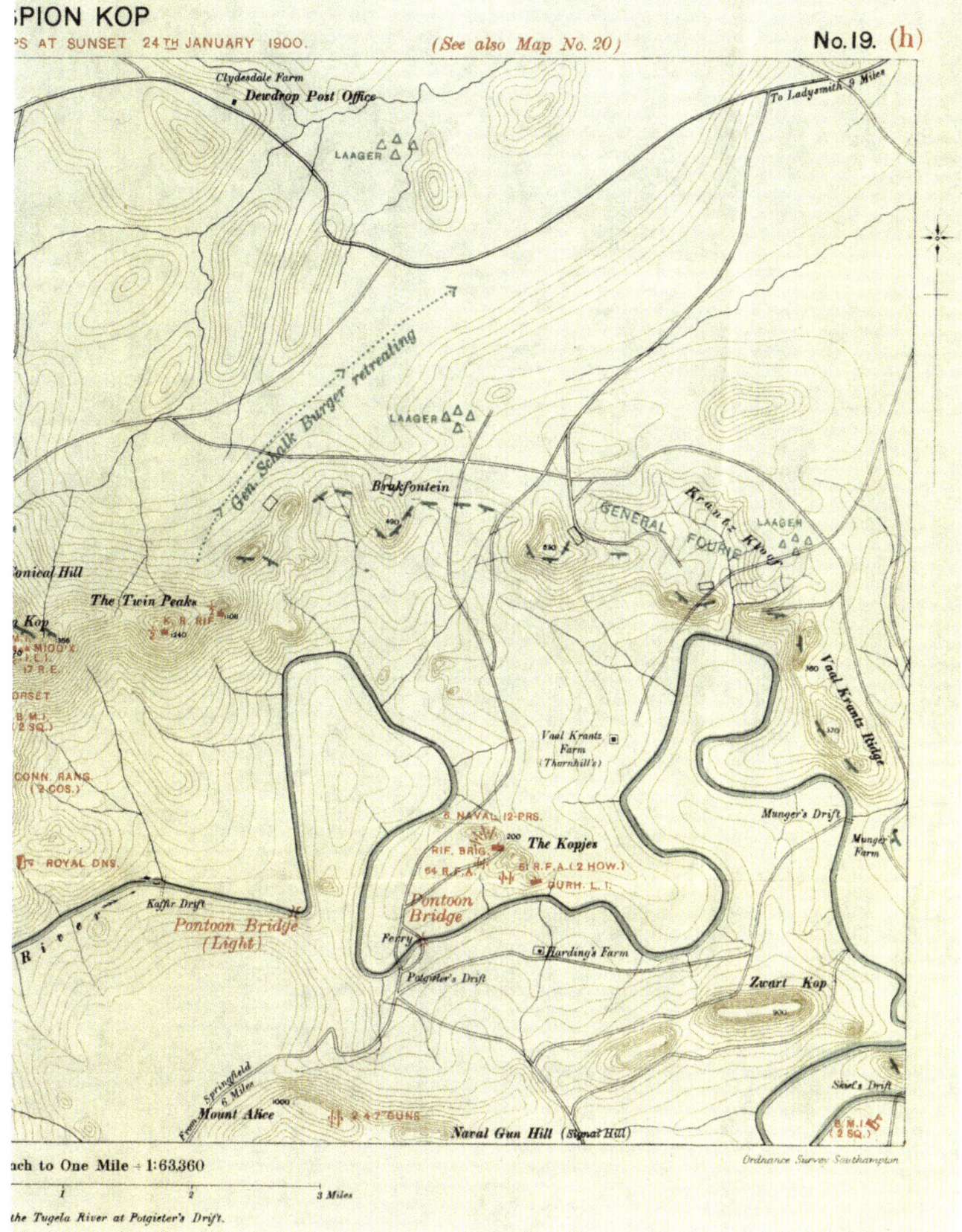

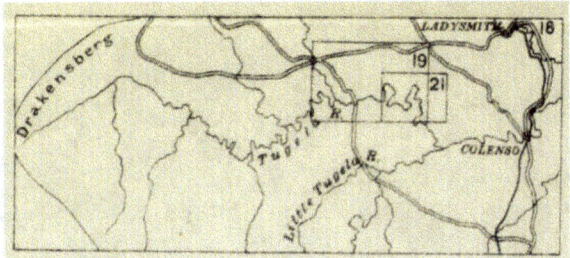

SPION KOP
AT SUNSET 25TH JANUARY 1900.

No. 19. (i)

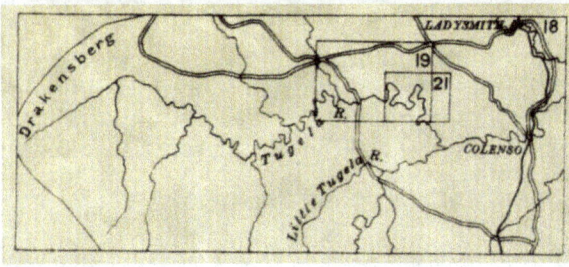

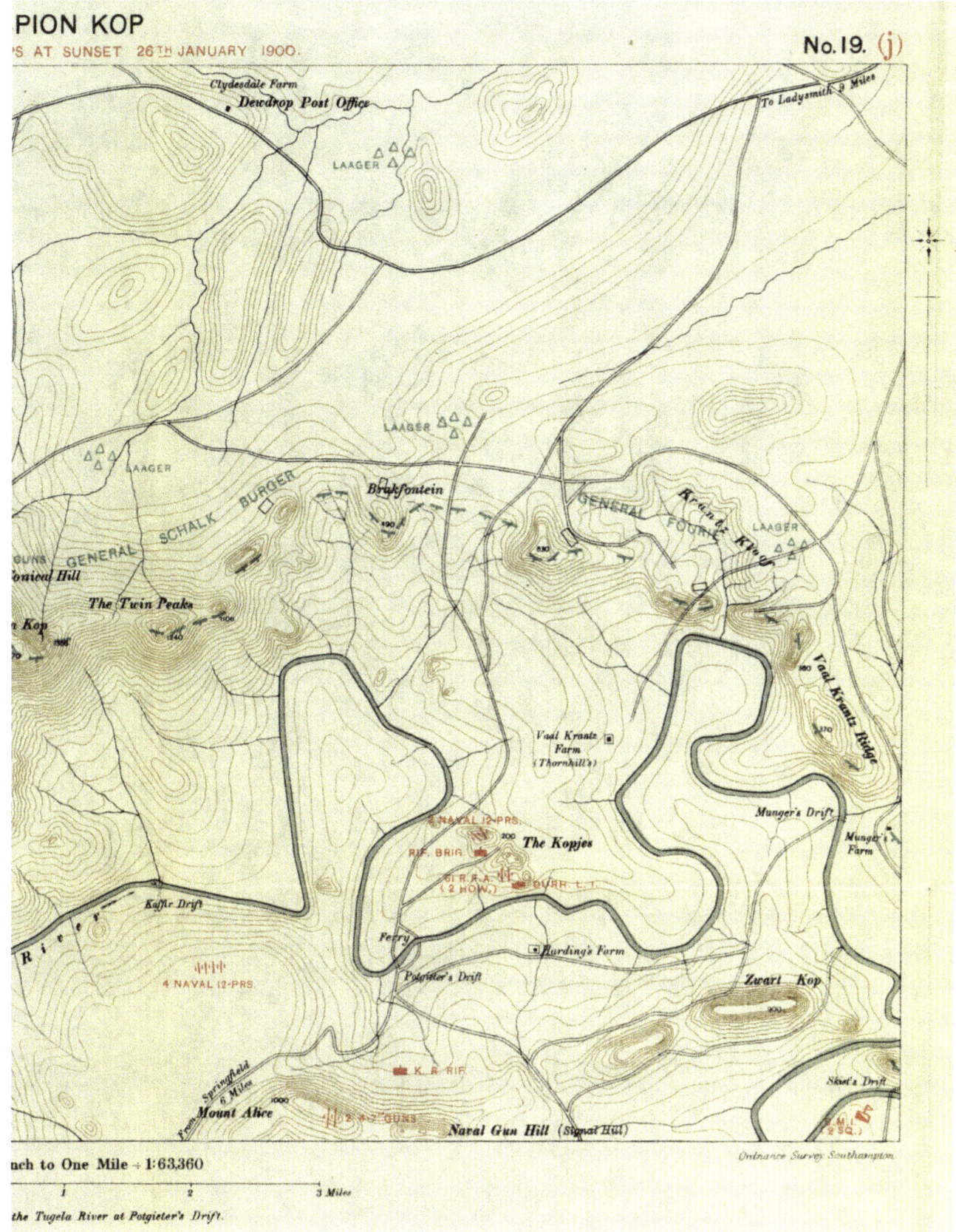

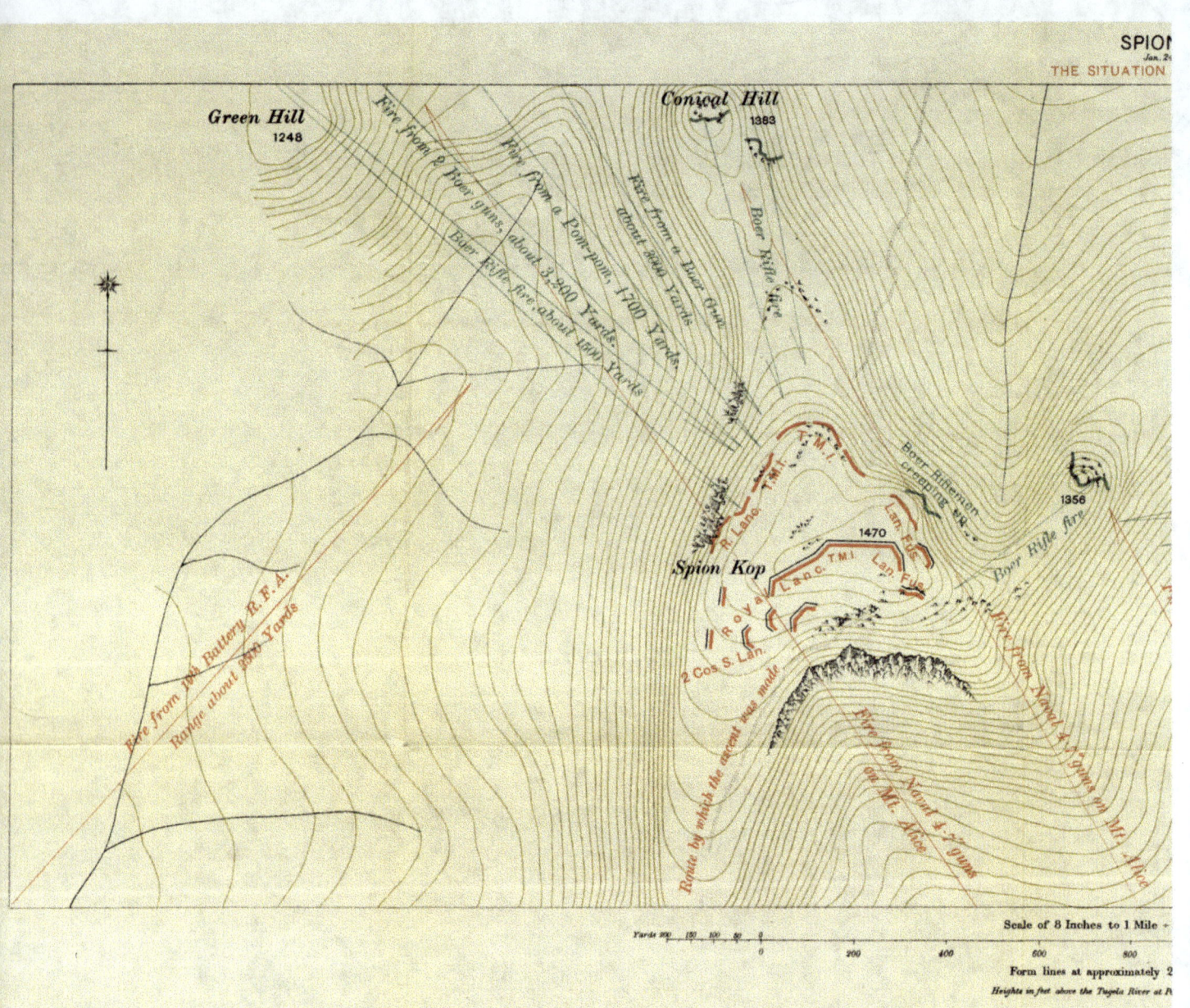

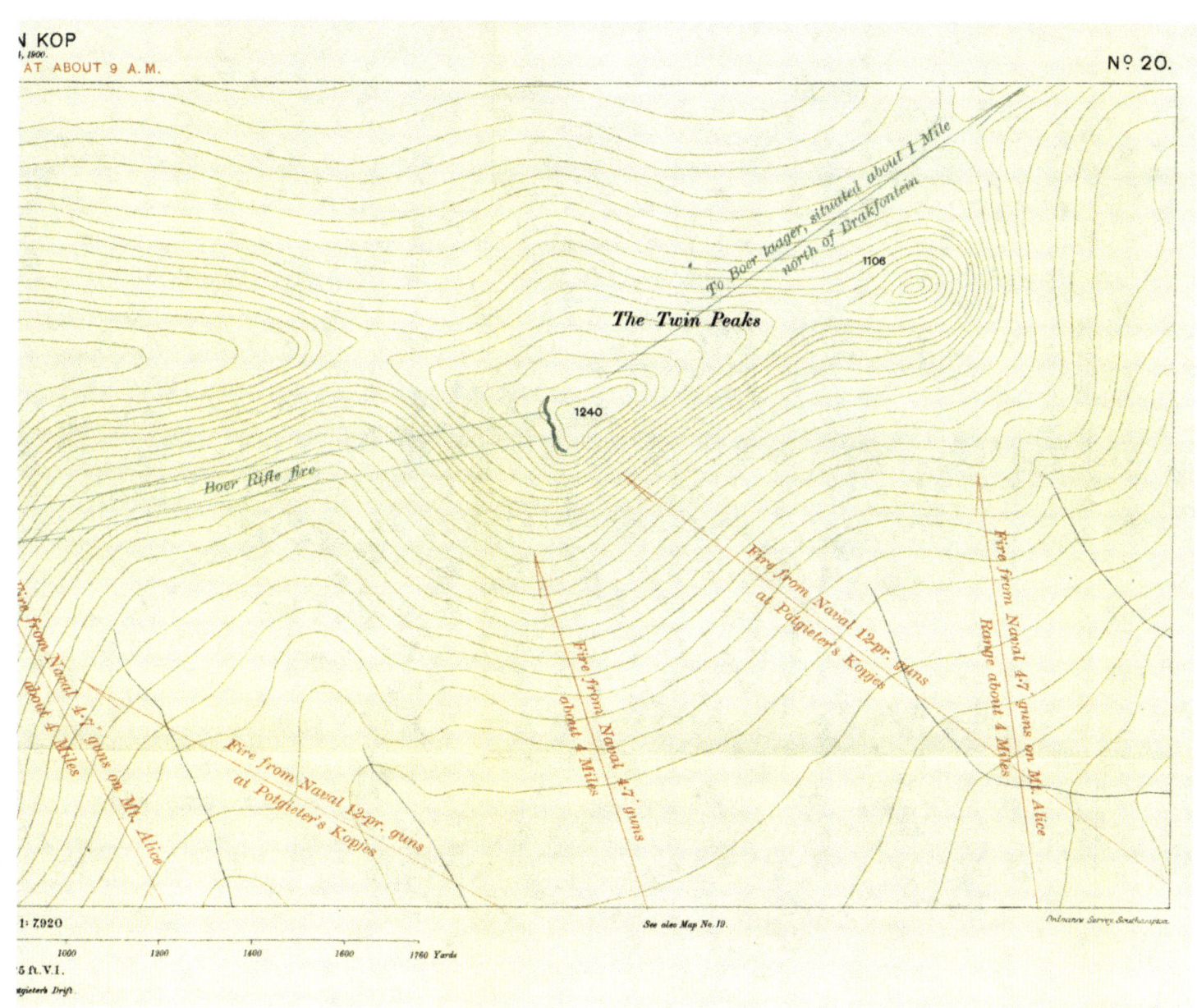

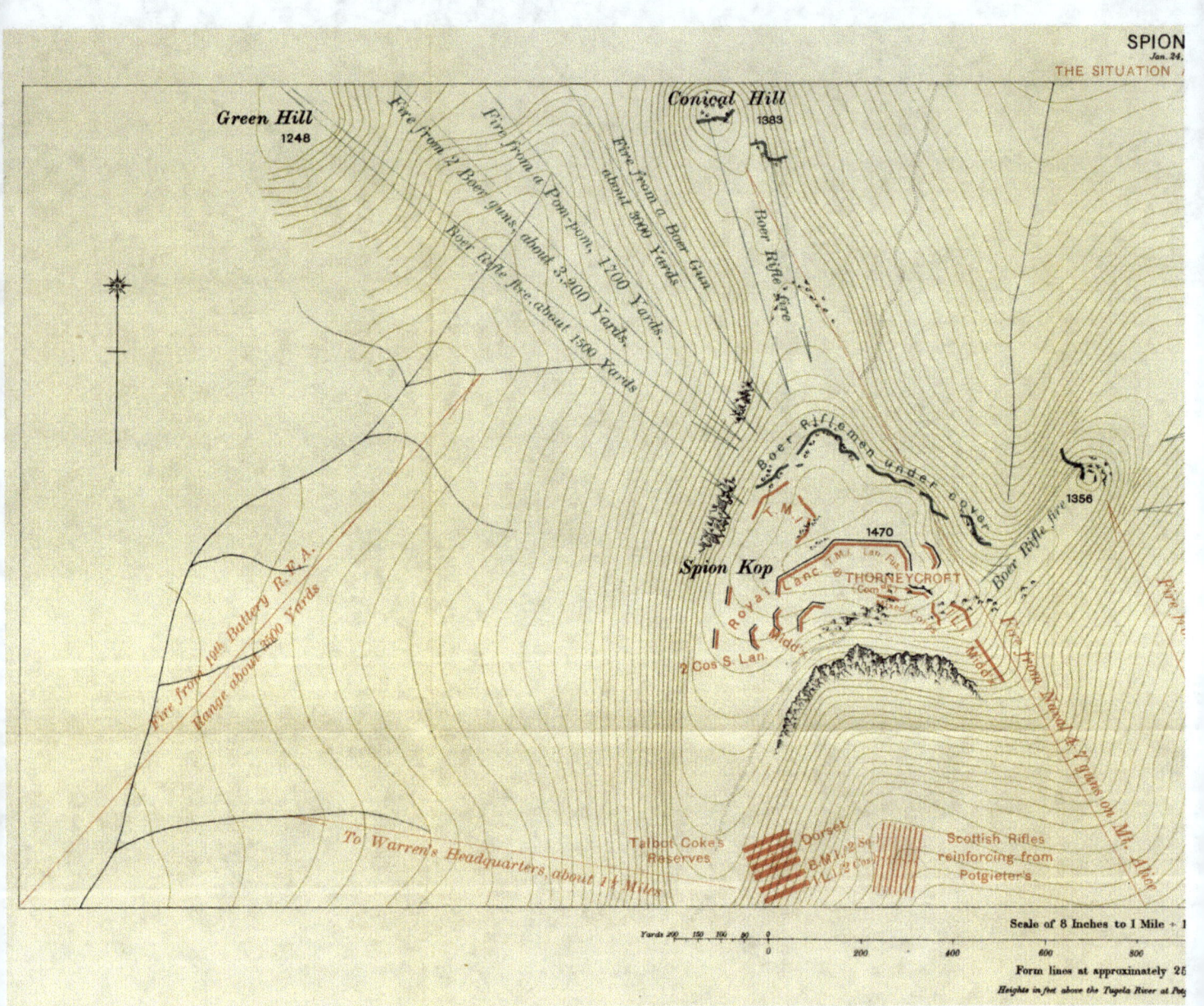

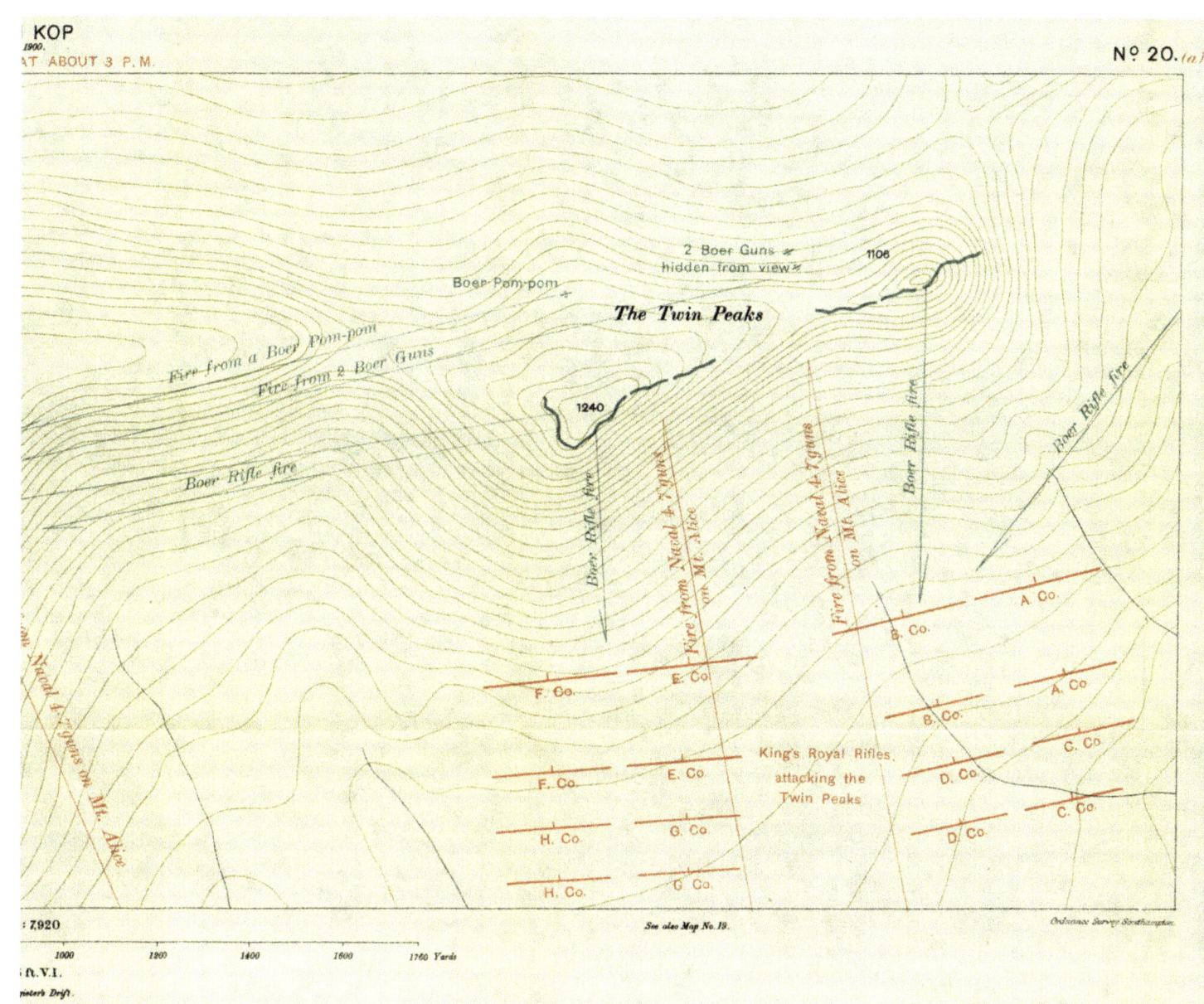

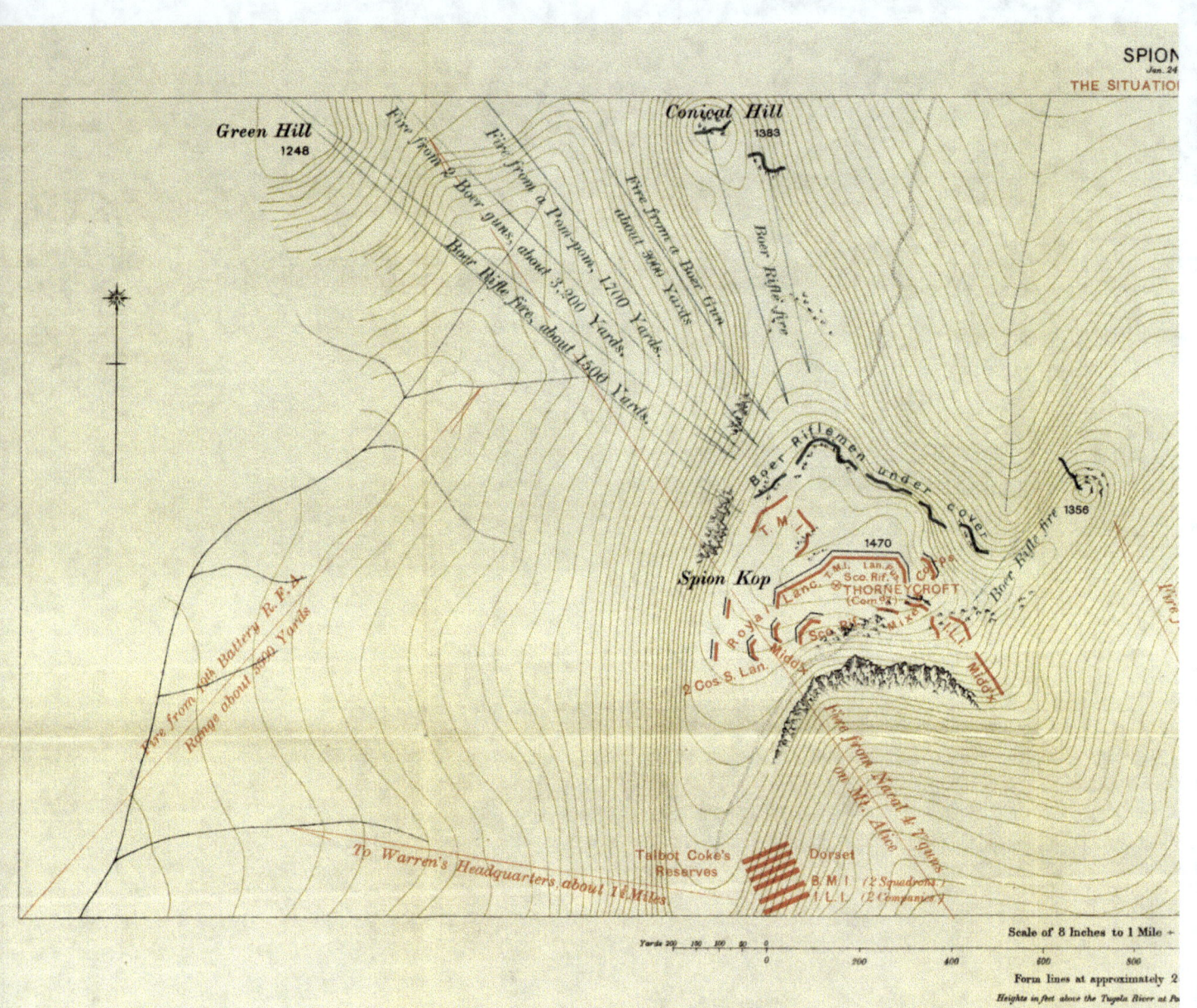

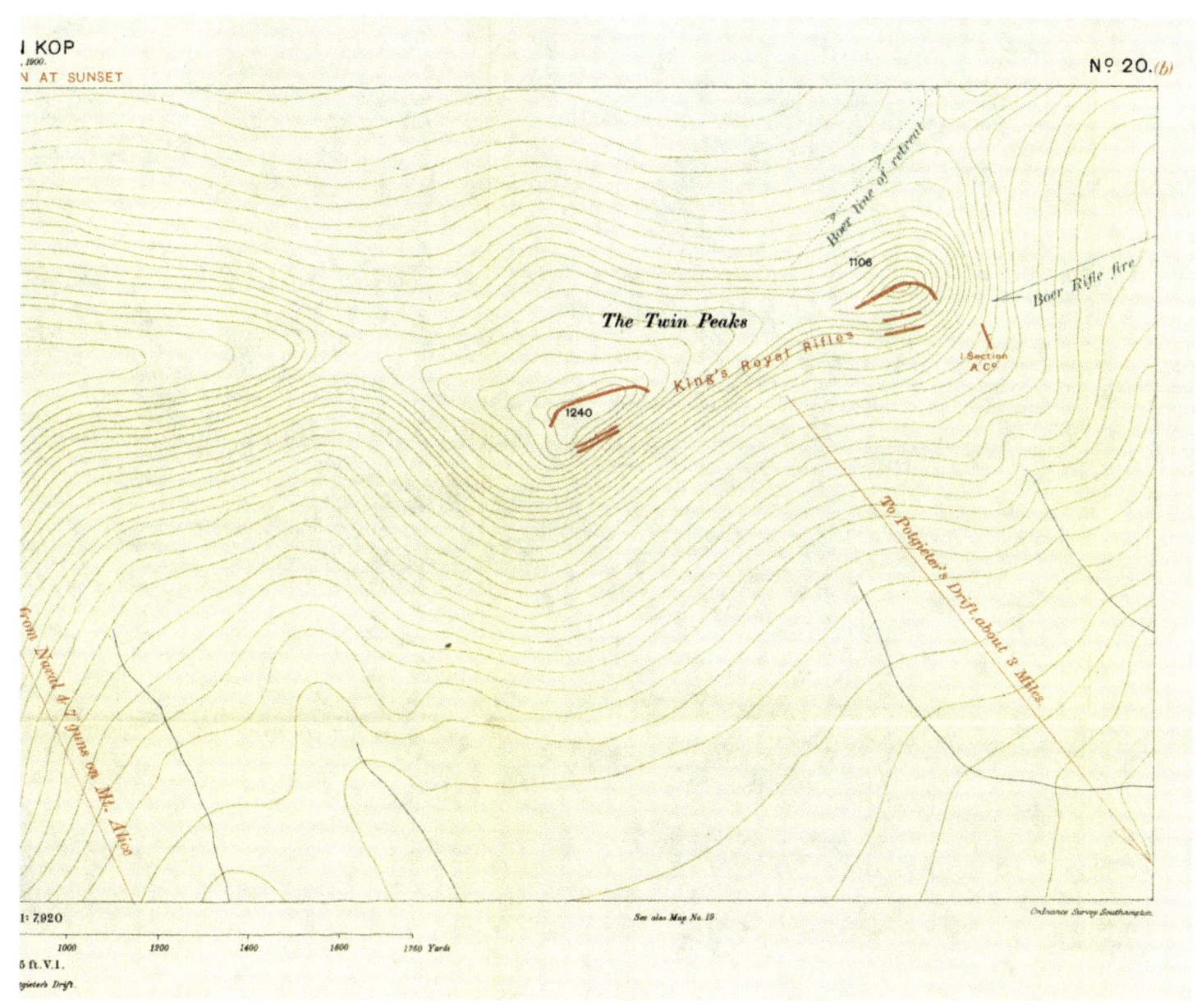

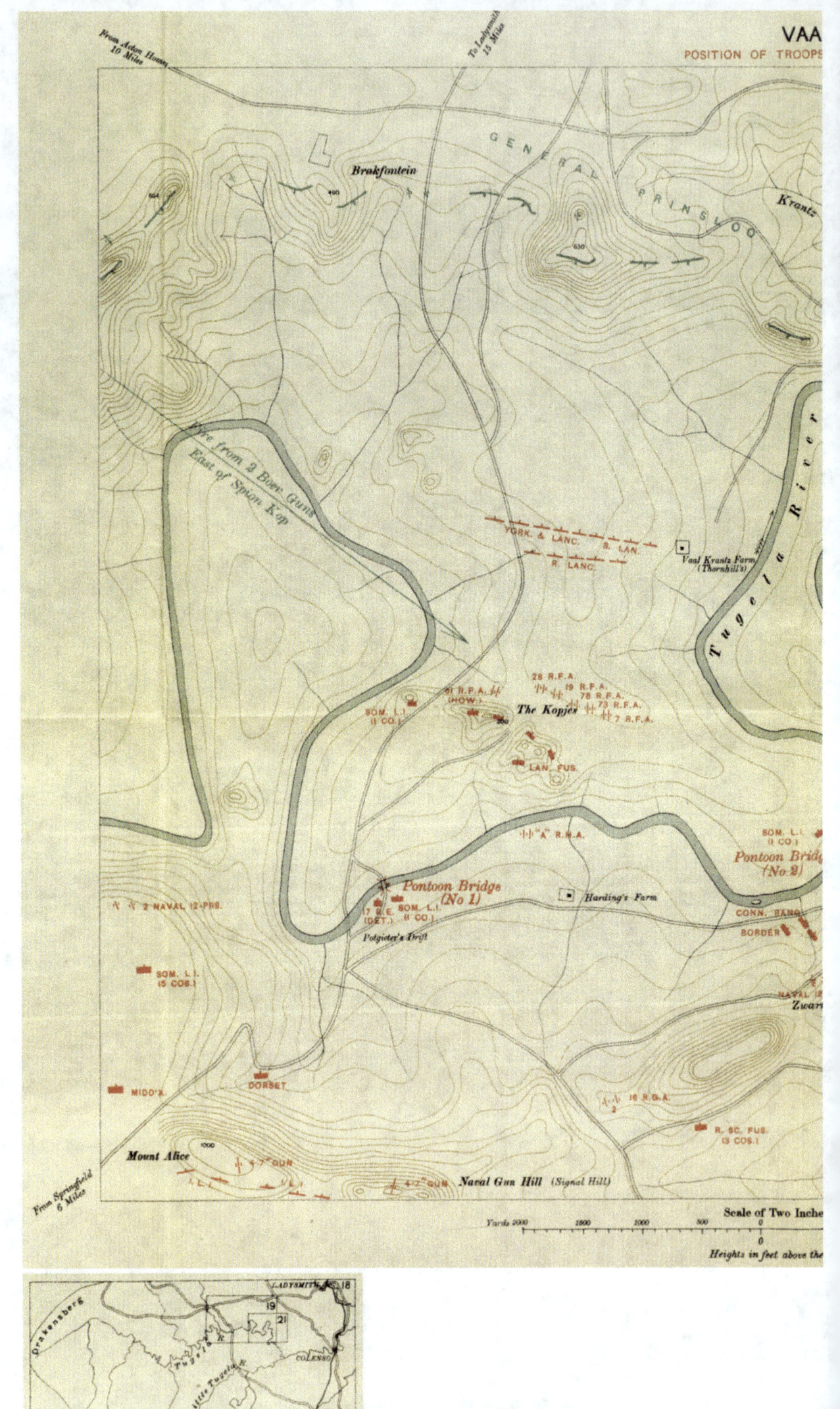

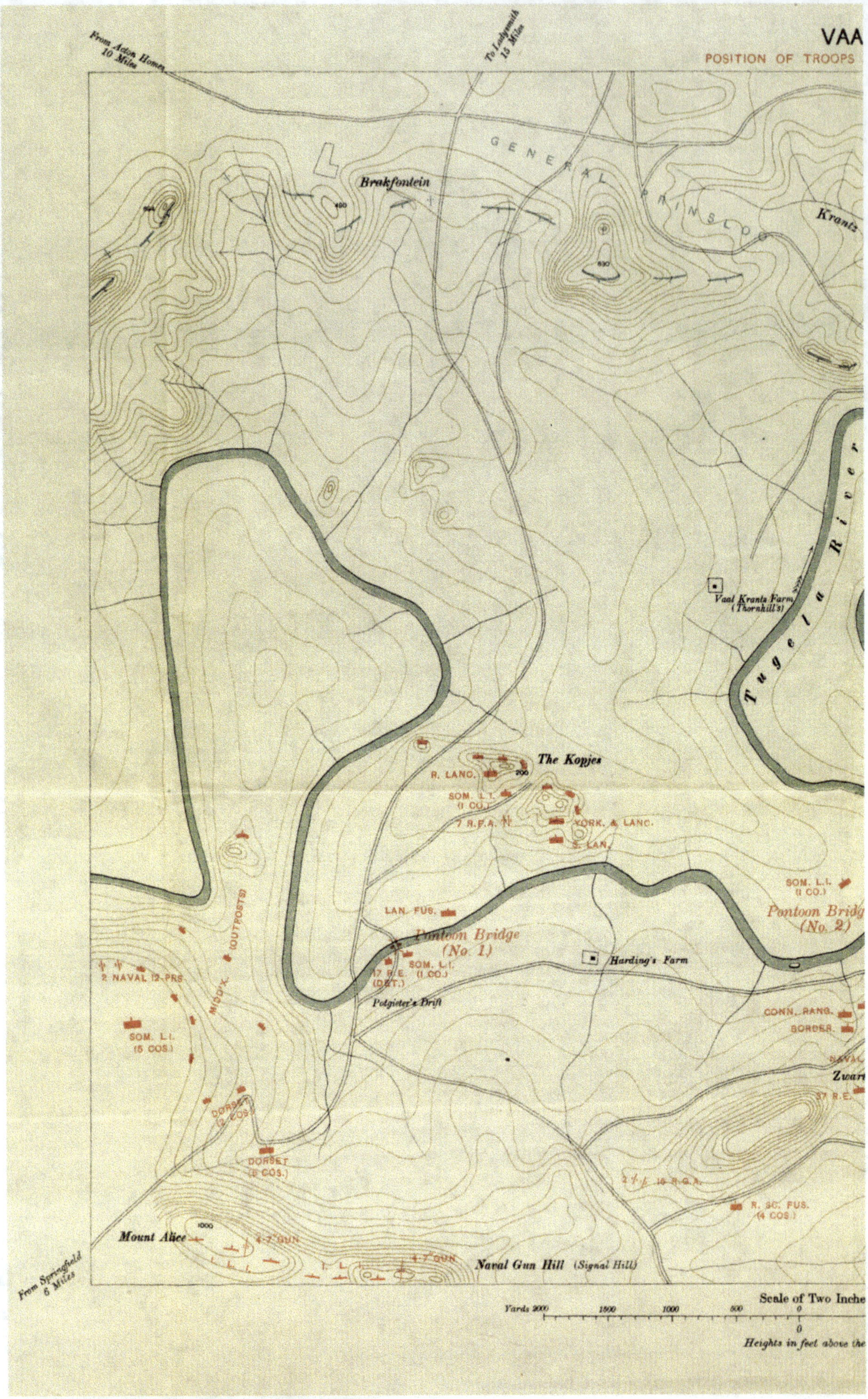

VAA
POSITION OF TROOPS
From Acton Homes 10 Miles
To Ladysmith 15 Miles
GENERAL PRINSLOO
Brakfontein
Krantz
Vaal Krantz Farm (Thornhill's)
Tugela River
The Kopjes
R. LANC.
SOM. L.I. (1 CO.)
7 R.F.A.
YORK. & LANC.
S. LAN.
SOM. L.I. (1 CO.)
Pontoon Bridge (No. 2)
LAN. FUS.
Pontoon Bridge (No. 1)
SOM. L.I. (1 CO.)
17 R.E. (DET.)
Potgieter's Drift
Harding's Farm
2 NAVAL 12-PRS
M'COY'S (OUTPOSTS)
SOM. L.I. (5 COS.)
CONN. RANG.
BORDER.
Zwart
37 R.E.
DORSET (2 COS.)
DORSET (6 COS.)
R. SC. FUS. (4 COS.)
Mount Alice
4·7" GUN
Naval Gun Hill (Signal Hill)
From Springfield 6 Miles
Scale of Two Inche
Yards 2000 1500 1000 500 0
Heights in feet above the

LADYSMITH
18
19
21
Drakensberg
Tugela R.
Little Tugela R.
COLENSO

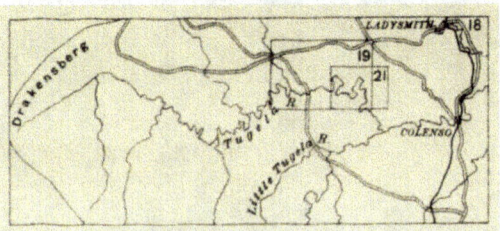

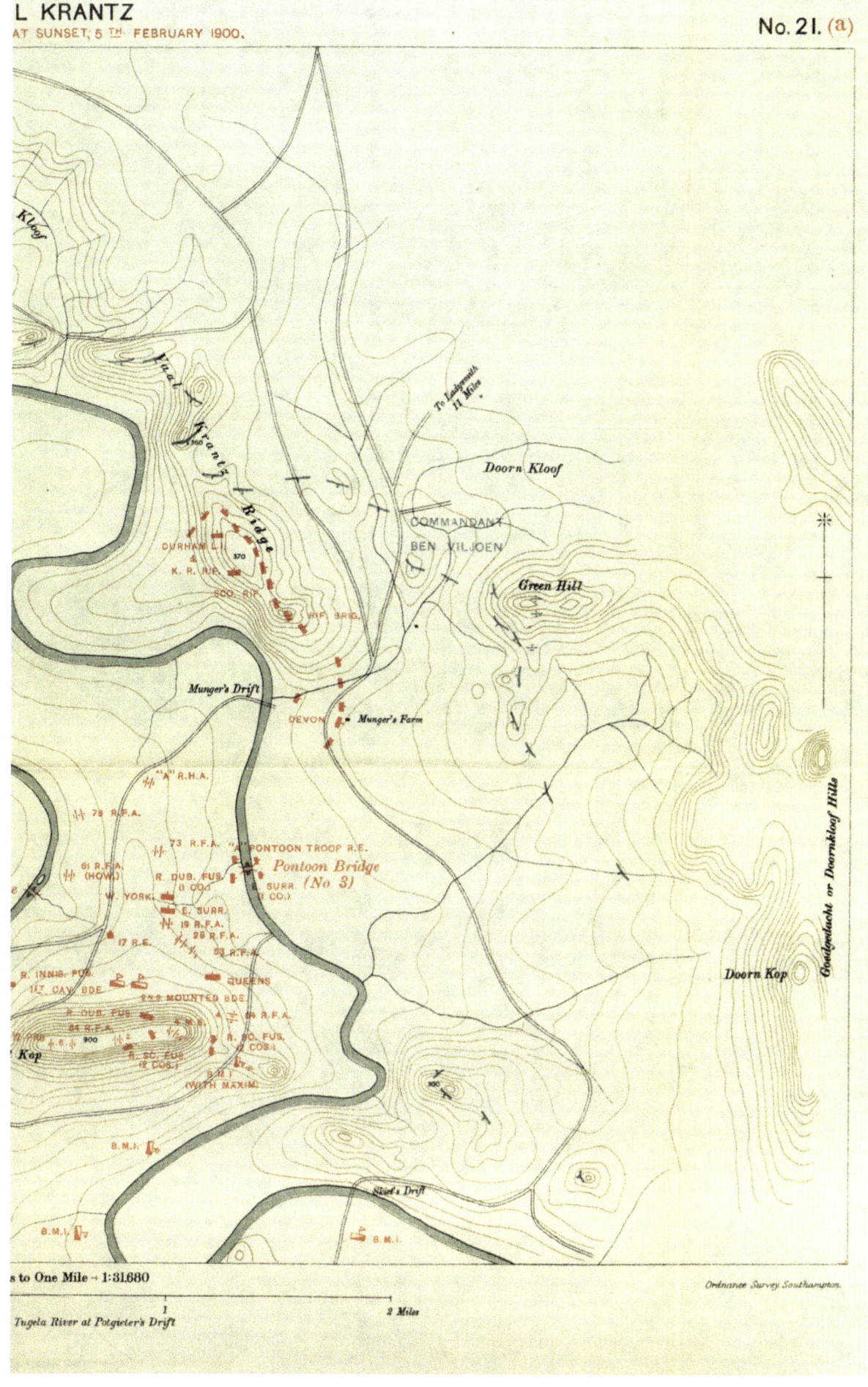

L KRANTZ
T MIDNIGHT, 6TH FEBRUARY 1900.

No. 21.(b)

Note
THE BRITISH GUNS TO THE NORTH OF ZWART KOP ARE SHOWN IN THE POSITIONS OCCUPIED AT DUSK 6TH FEB., AND AT DAYBREAK 7TH FEB., THE INTERVENING PERIOD WAS SPENT IN BIVOUAC UNDER THE NORTHERN SLOPES OF ZWART KOP

… L KRANTZ
… SUNSET, 7TH FEBRUARY 1900.

No. 21. (C)

Kloof

Vaal Krantz Ridge

QUEENS
DEVON
E. SURR.
W. YORK.

Pontoon Bridge (No. 4)
PONTOON TROOP R.E.

Munger's Drift

CONN. RANG.
Munger's Farm

To Ladysmith 11 Miles

Doorn Kloof

COMMANDANT BEN VILJOEN

Green Hill

GENERALS LOUIS BOTHA
AND
LUKAS MEYER

19 R.F.A.
73 & 78 R.F.A.
28 R.F.A.   63 R.F.A.
YORK. & LANC. (OUTPOSTS)
61 R.F.A. (HOW.)
NAVAL 12-PRS.
R. DUB. FUS. (1 CO.)
37 R.E.
RIF. BRIG.
Pontoon Bridge (No. 3.)
R. INNIS. FUS. (6 COS.)
17 R.E.
16 R.G.A.

K. R. RIF.   DURHAM L.I.
SCO. RIF.
BORDER   R. DUB. FUS. (7 COS.)
R. SC. FUS. (1 CO.)
LANC.   M.B.   64 R.F.A.
12-PRS.   900   R. SC. FUS. (2 COS.)
64 R.F.A.
R. SC. FUS. (1 CO.)
B.M.I. (WITH MAXIM)

Kop

S.M.I.
2ND MOUNTED BDE.

S.M.I.

Skiet's Drift

S.M.I.

Goedgedacht or Doornkloof Hills

Doorn Kop
6" GUN (LONG TOM)

Scale … s to One Mile = 1:31,680

0 — 1 — 2 Miles

Tugela River at Potgieter's Drift

Ordnance Survey, Southampton.

Fraser's Drift
MODDER RIVER
River
Seven Fountains
Bosch Pan
JACOBSDAL
Middlebosch
Emmaus
Petrusburg
Boesmanspan
To Bloemfontein 45 Miles
Bosch Kop
Veal Kop
Gruis Kop
HONEYNEST KLOOF
Wegdraai Drift
Kromkuil
Rooidam
Blauwboschpan
7th. DIVISION
2 a.m. 15th. FEB.
march of LUBBE 13th. FEB.
Vander Merwes Dam
Vaalpan
Wit Dam
ENSLIN
Lanshoek
C. DE WET 12th. FEB.
6th. DIVISION 13th. FEB.
Poortje
C. DE WET 11th. FEB.
Blaauwbank
Blaauwbank Drift
Waterval Drift
Riet River
6th. DIVISION & M.I. 12th. FEB.
Randam
GRASPAN
Waterval Hill
De Kiel's Drift
Winterhoek
C. DE WET & A. CRONJE 12th. to 14th. FEB.
Honing Berg
Poortjesdam
From Hopetown 34 Miles
Doornhoek
Koffyfontein
Uitdraai
Boujespan
Swenkpan
Pandam
Scale of One Inch to Four Miles = 1 : 253,440
Miles 4 3 2 1 0 4 8 12 Miles
Heights in Feet above Sea-level
To Fauresmith 18 Miles
Ordnance Survey, Southampton.

26
22
25
Boshof
KIMBERLEY
29
23
24
26
27
Modder R.
JACOBSDAL
BLOEMFONTEIN

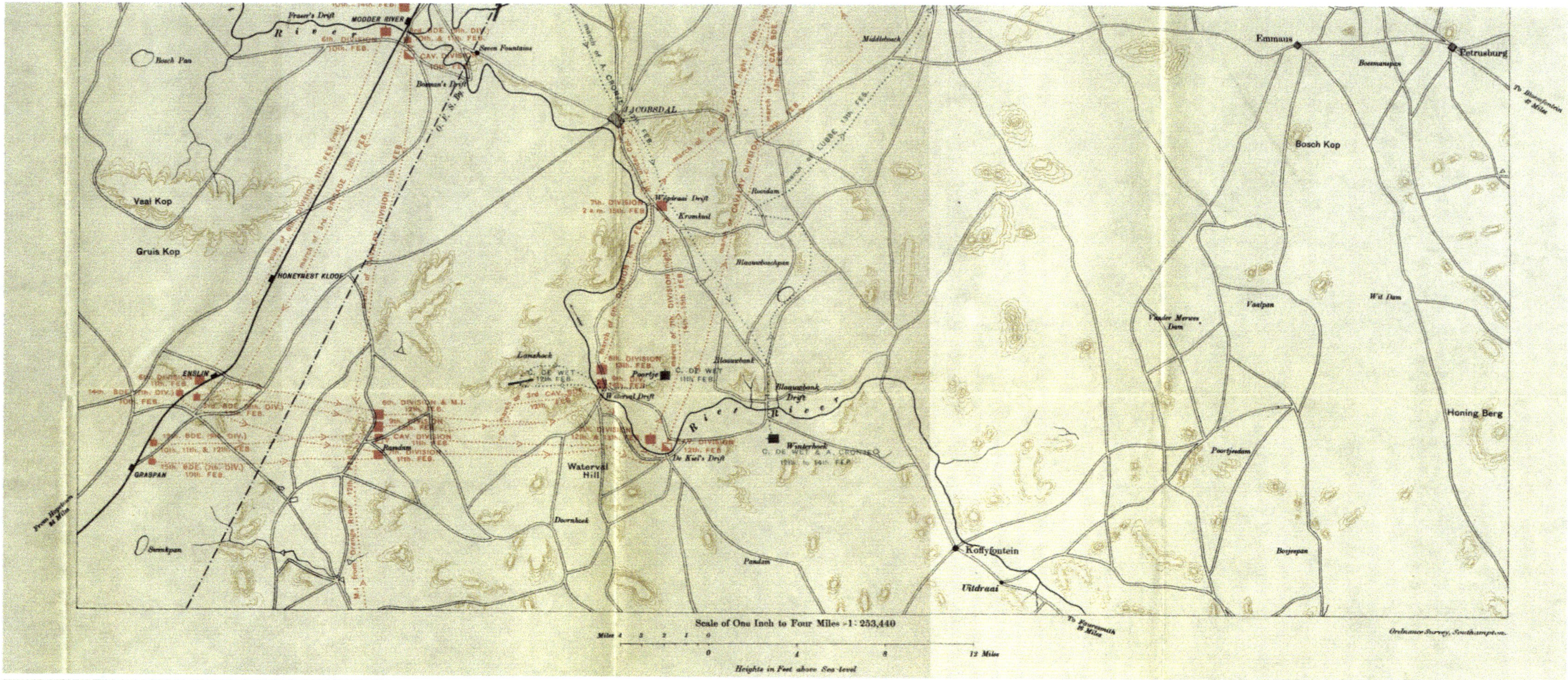

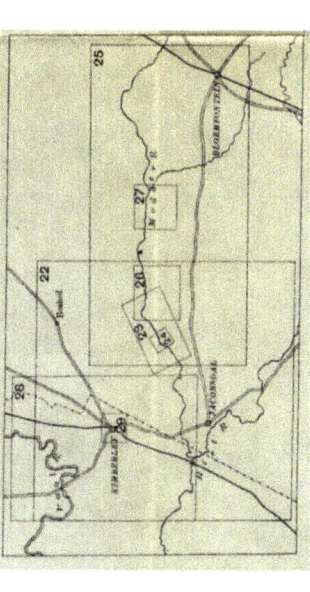

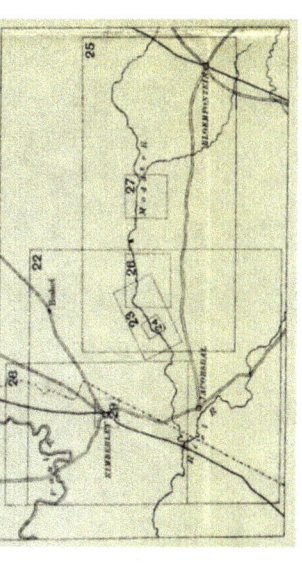

MODDER RIVER
Fraser's Drift
Seven Fountains
Bosch Pan
JACOBSDAL
14th. BDE. 17th. FEB.
15th. BDE. 16th. & 17th. FEB.
13th. BDE. 16th. FEB.
14th. BDE. 16th. FEB.
Wegdraai Drift
3rd. BDE. 16th. FEB.
Kromkuil
Middlebosch
Roodam
Blaauwboschpan
Vaal Kop
Gruis Kop
HONEYNEST KLOOF
ENSLIN
GRASPAN
Swinkpan
Randam
Lanahoek
Poortje
Waterval Drift
Waterval Hill
Doornhoek
De Kiel's Drift
Riet River
Blaauwbank
Blaauwbank Drift
DE WET & A. CRONJE 16th. FEB.
Winterhoek
Pandam
DE WET & A. CRONJE 17th. FEB.
Koffyfontein
Uitdraai
Emmaus
Petrusburg
Boesmanspan
Bosch Kop
Wit Dam
Vander Merwes Dam
Vaalpan
Honing Berg
Poortjesdam
Boyespan
Scale of One Inch to Four Miles -1: 253,440
Miles 4 3 2 1 0 4 8 12 Miles
Heights in Feet above Sea-level
Ordnance Survey, Southampton.

28
22
25
KIMBERLEY
29
23
24
26
27
JACOBSDAL
BLOEMFONTEIN

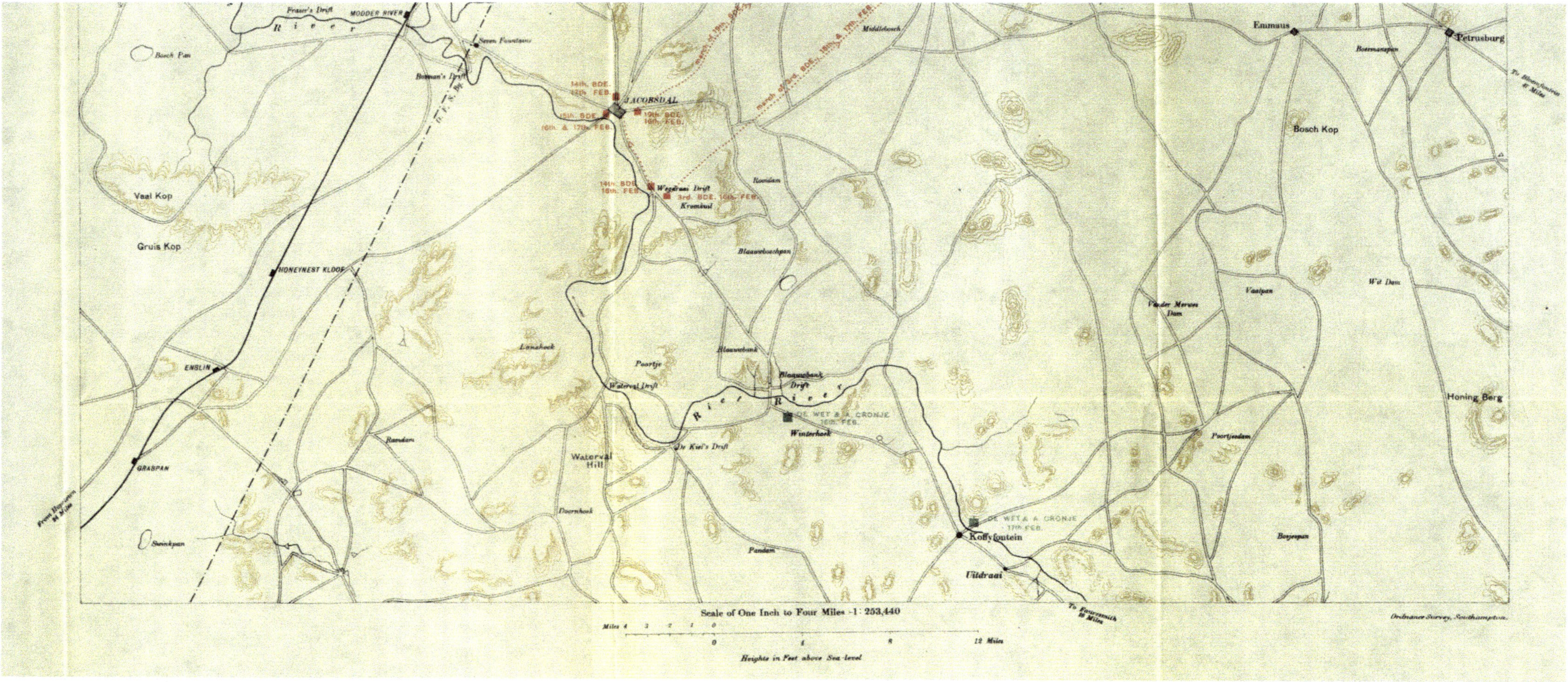

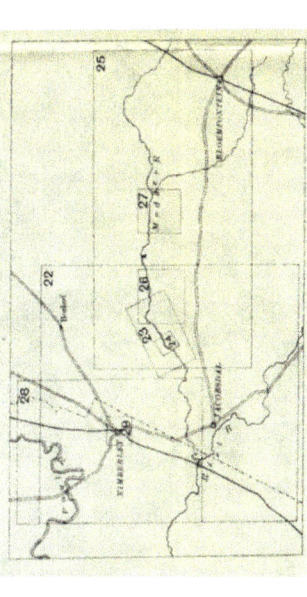

PAARDEB
SITUATION ABOUT 8 a.m.
BROADWOOD
G & P R.H.A.
Gun Hill
Paardeberg
LAAGER
Wolve Kraal
Paardeberg Drift
Vendutie Drift
Vanderberg Drift
2nd. & 7th. M. I.
19th. BDE.
HIGHLAND BDE. in file
82 R.F.A.
Signal Hill
OXF. L.I.
W. RID.
YORK
BUFFS (4 Cos.)
GLO'STER (2 Cos.)
WELSH (2 Cos.)
KITCHENER'S HORSE
Kraals
9th. DIVISION (Bivouac. 17th. FEB.)
D.C.L.I.
9th. DIVISION (Baggage)
BUFFS (4 Cos.)
GLO'STER (3 Cos.)
6th. DIVISION (Baggage)
6th. DIVISION (Bivouac. 17th. FEB.)
WELSH (5 Cos.)
ESSEX
Kitchener's Kopje
KITCHENER'S HORSE
Osfontein
HANNAY
Damfontein
Pan
From Kimberley
From Jacobsdal 24 Miles
From Koffyfontein
To Petrusburg 14 Miles
Scale of One Inch to O
Form lines at approxi

28
22
25
23
26
27
24
29
KIMBERLEY
JACOBSDAL
BLOEMFONTEIN
Modder R.

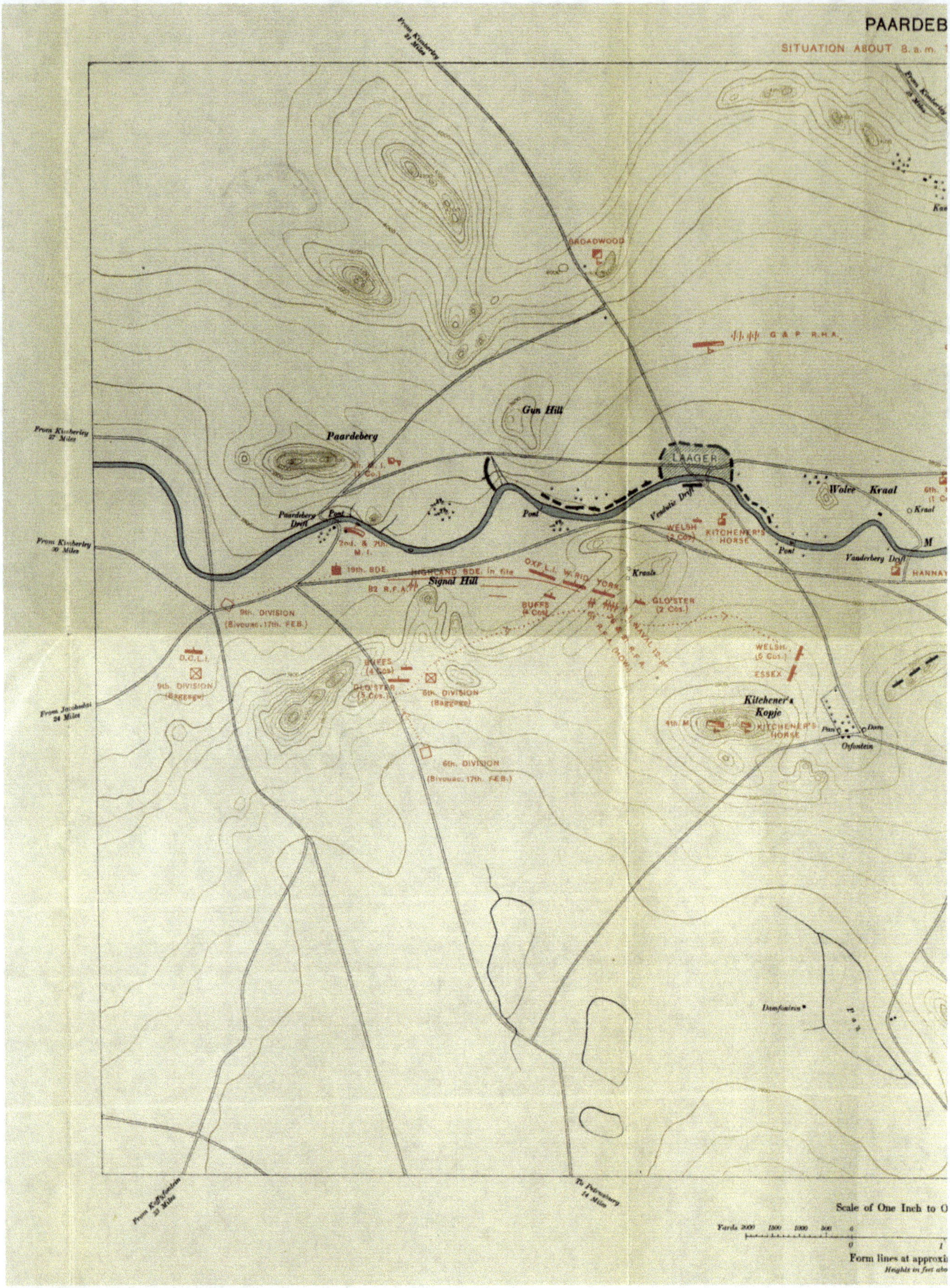

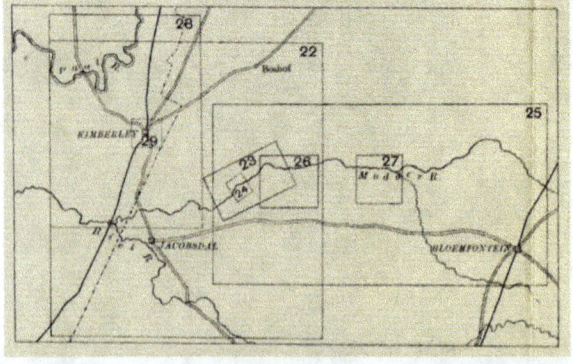

Protected Bivouac and Works
of the 14th Brigade and 9th (Field) Company R.E.
NEAR PAARDEBERG
21st to 27th February 1900.

No. 24.

Note:—
British Works. Red
Boer do. Green

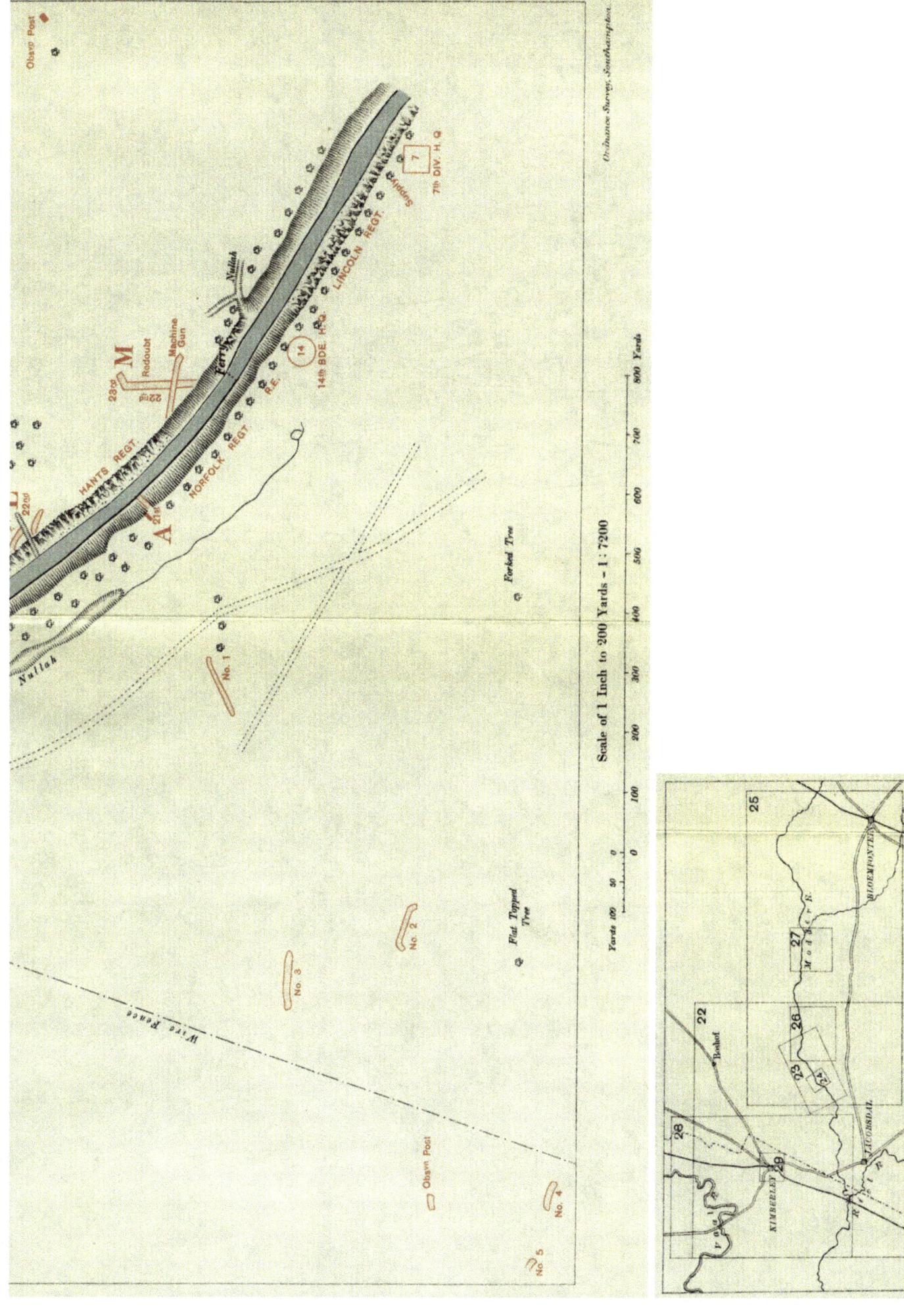

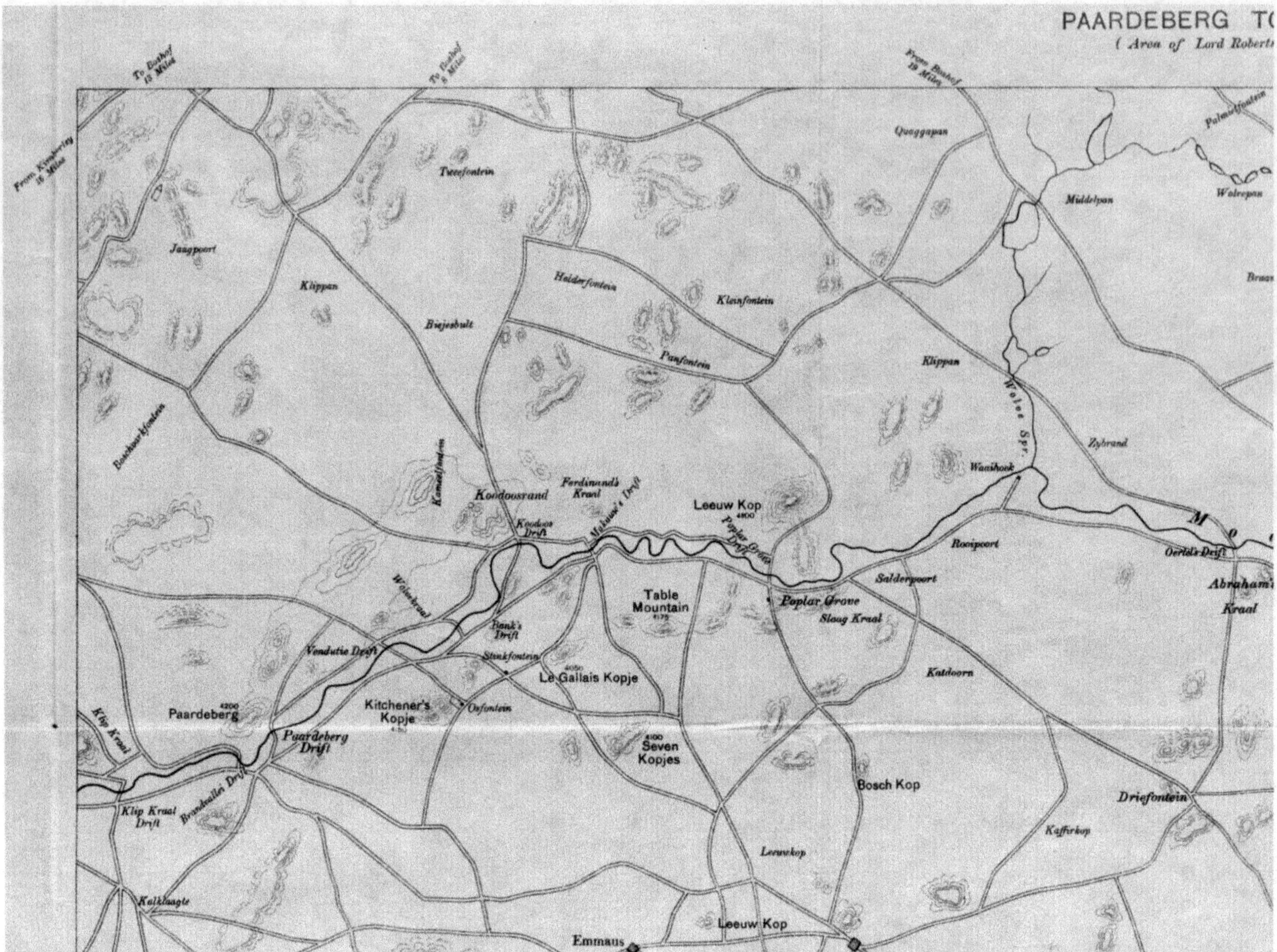
PAARDEBERG TO
(Area of Lord Roberts
To Boshof 15 Miles
To Boshof 8 Miles
From Boshof 19 Miles
From Kimberley 16 Miles
Quaggapan
Palmietfontein
Tweefontein
Middelpan
Wolvepan
Jaagpoort
Klippan
Biejesbult
Helderfontein
Kleinfontein
Panfontein
Klippan
Modder Spr.
Zybrand
Waaihoek
Koodoosrand
Ferdinand's Kraal
Koodoos Drift
Makauw's Drift
Leeuw Kop
4800
Poplar Grove Drift
Rooipoort
Oertel's Drift
Abraham's Kraal
Salderpoort
Table Mountain
Poplar Grove
Slaag Kraal
Vendutie Drift
Bank's Drift
Stinkfontein
Le Gallais Kopje
Katdoorn
Paardeberg
4200
Kitchener's Kopje
Paardeberg Drift
Seven Kopjes
4100
Klip Kraal
Klip Kraal Drift
Brandvallei Drift
Bosch Kop
Driefontein
Kaffirkop
Leeuwkop
Kalklaagte
Leeuw Kop
Emmaus
Petrusburg
Boesmanspan
From Jacobsdal 10½ Miles
Rietfontein
Uitval
Bosch Kop
Doornkop
Bester's Put
Drickop
Doorn Kop
Wit Dam
Katdoornpan
Vaalpan
Olivenberg
Van der Merwe Dam
Oorland's Poort
Zwart Randsdam
Welkom
Van Heerdens
From Koffyfontein 12 Miles
Scale of One Inch to
Miles 4 3 2 1 0
Heights in fe

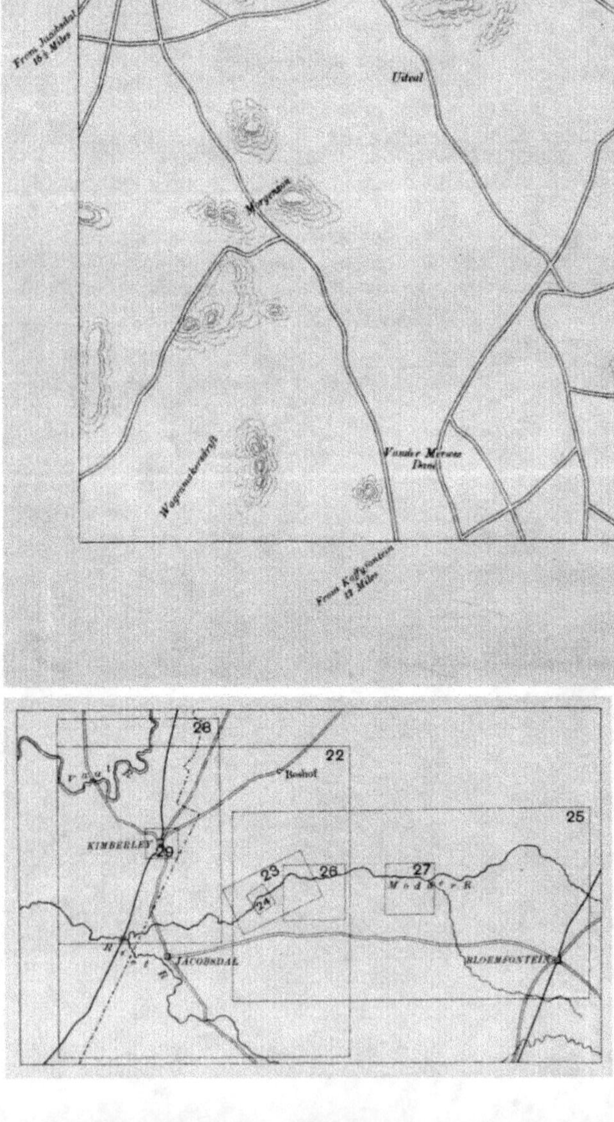
28
22
Boshof
25
KIMBERLEY
29
23
26
27
24
Modder R.
JACOBSDAL
BLOEMFONTEIN

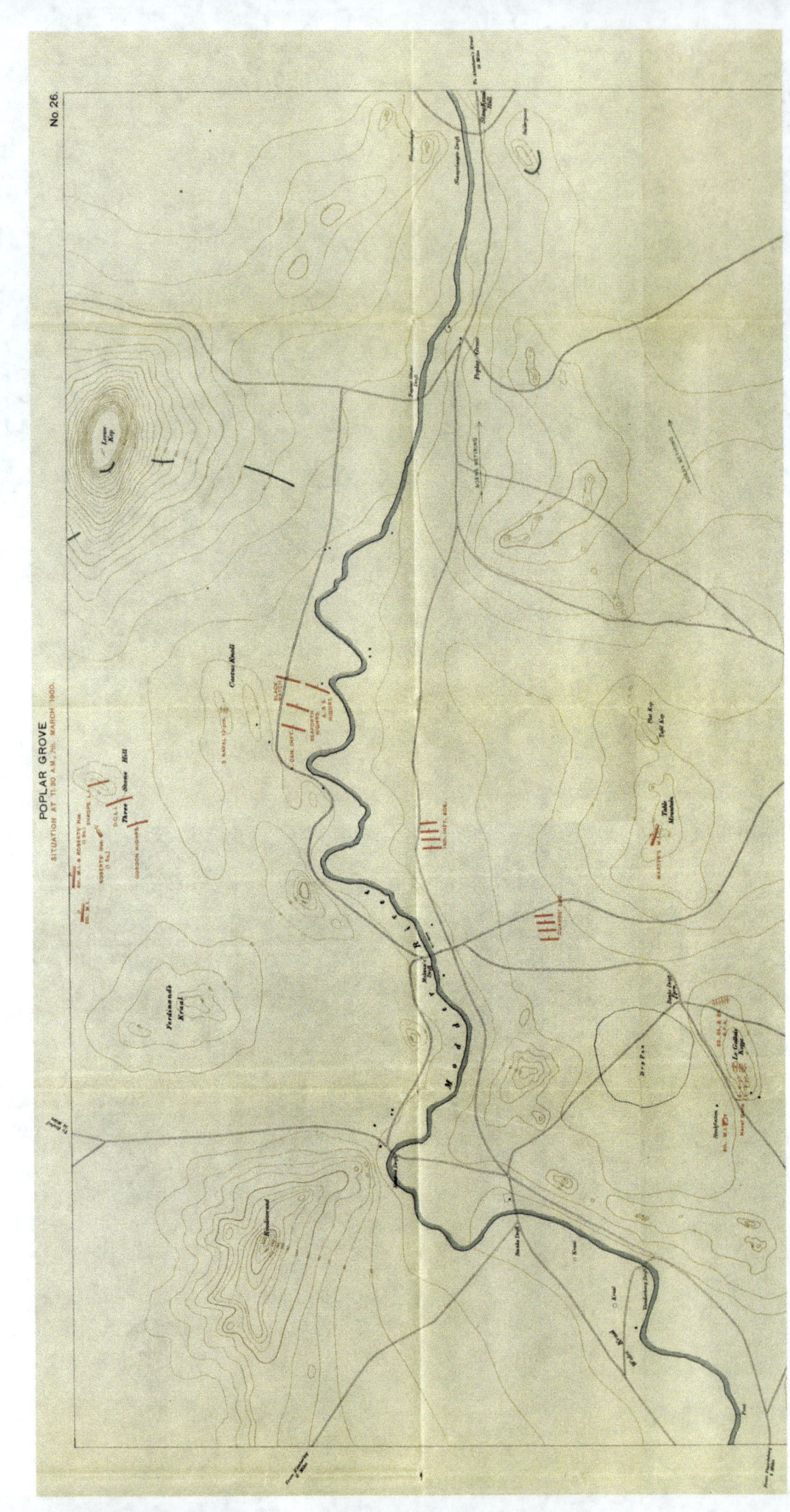

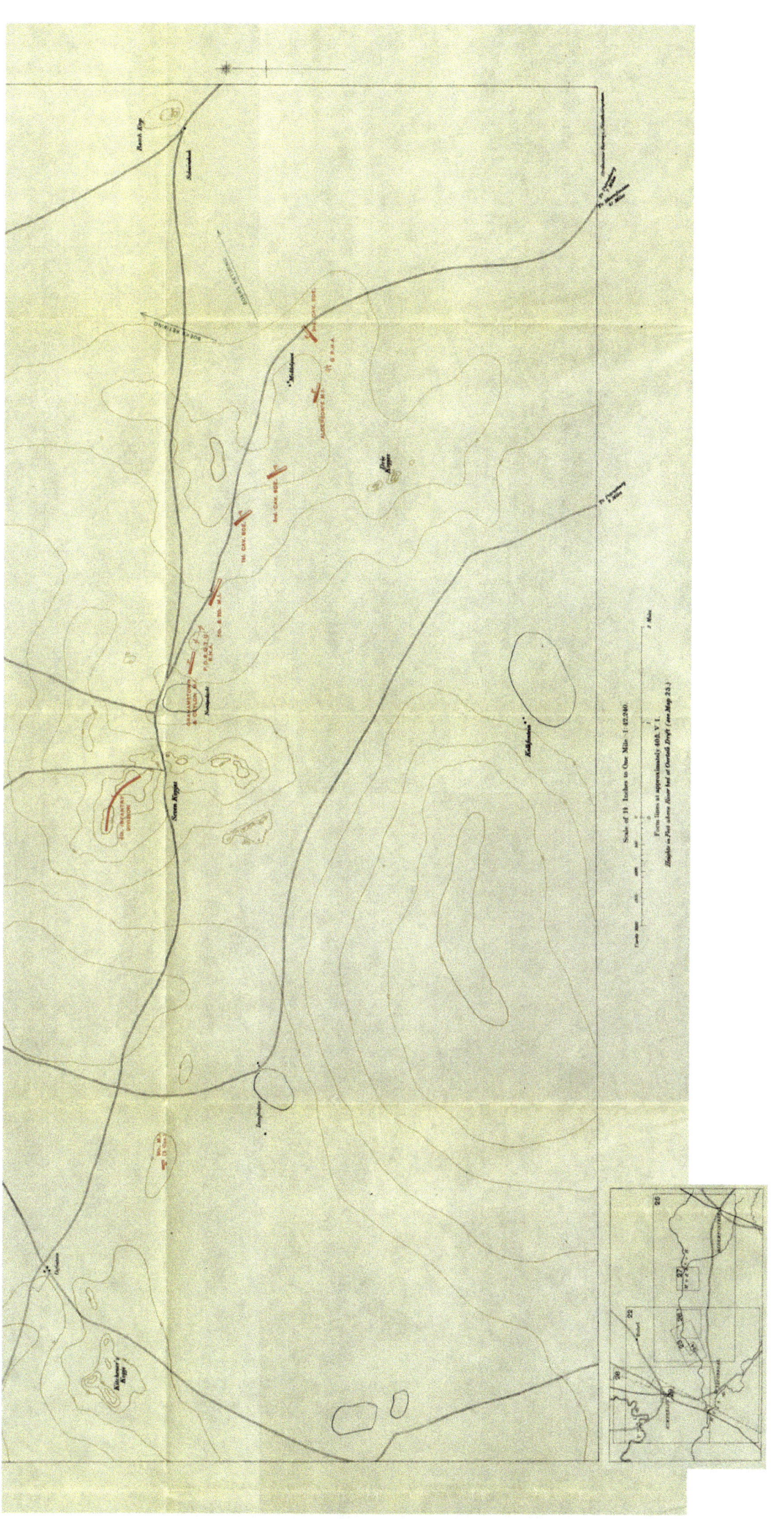

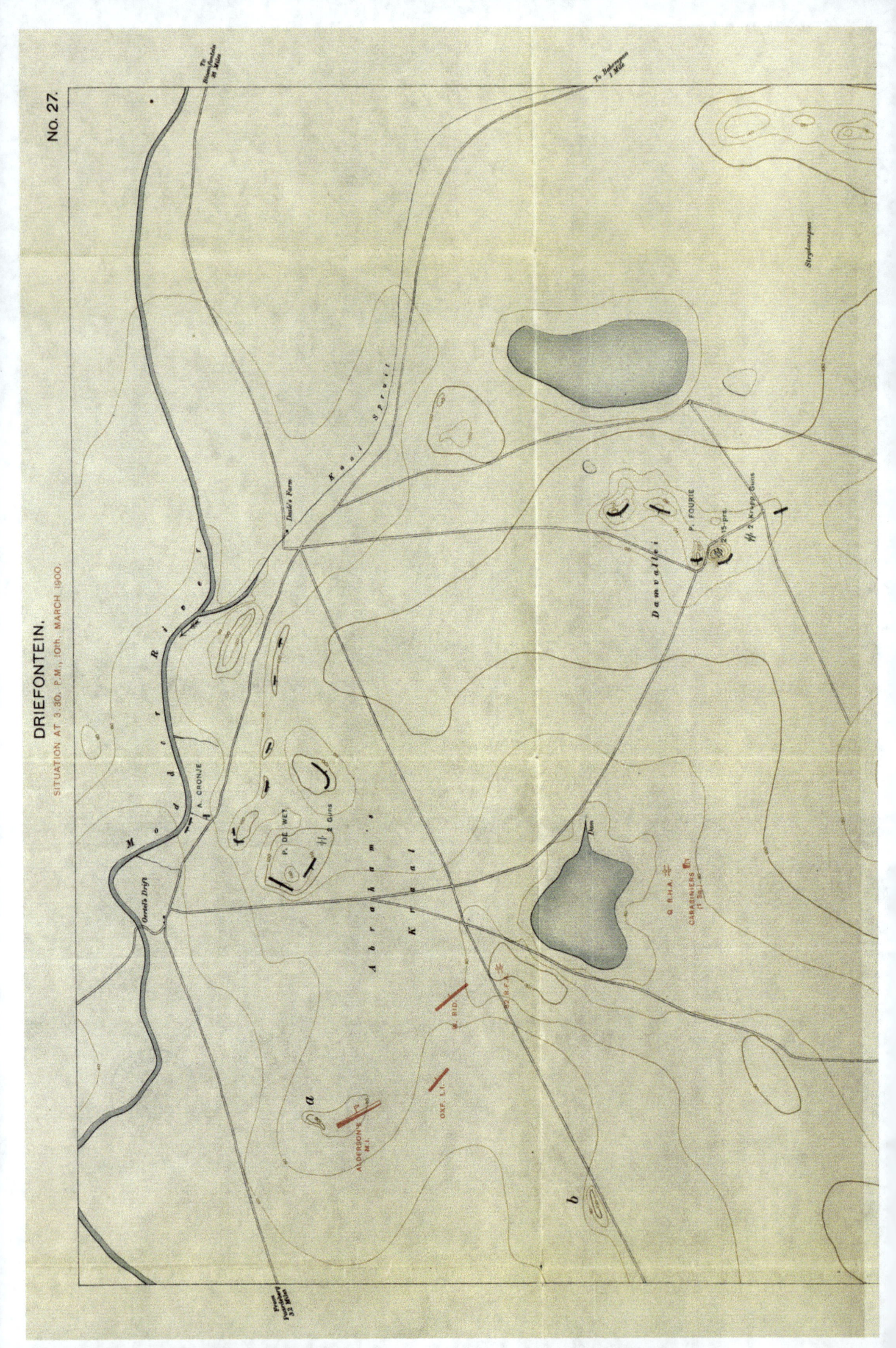

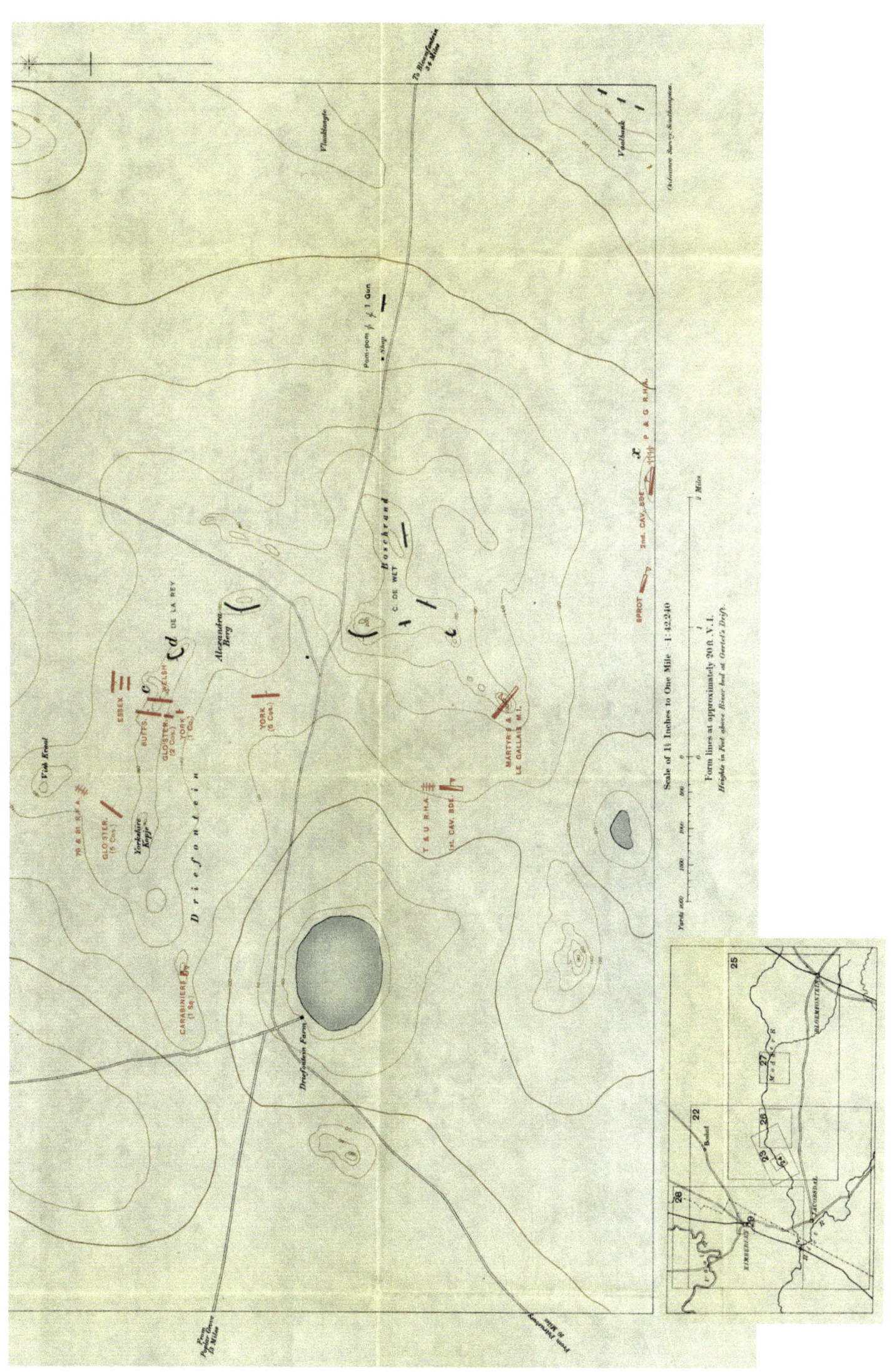

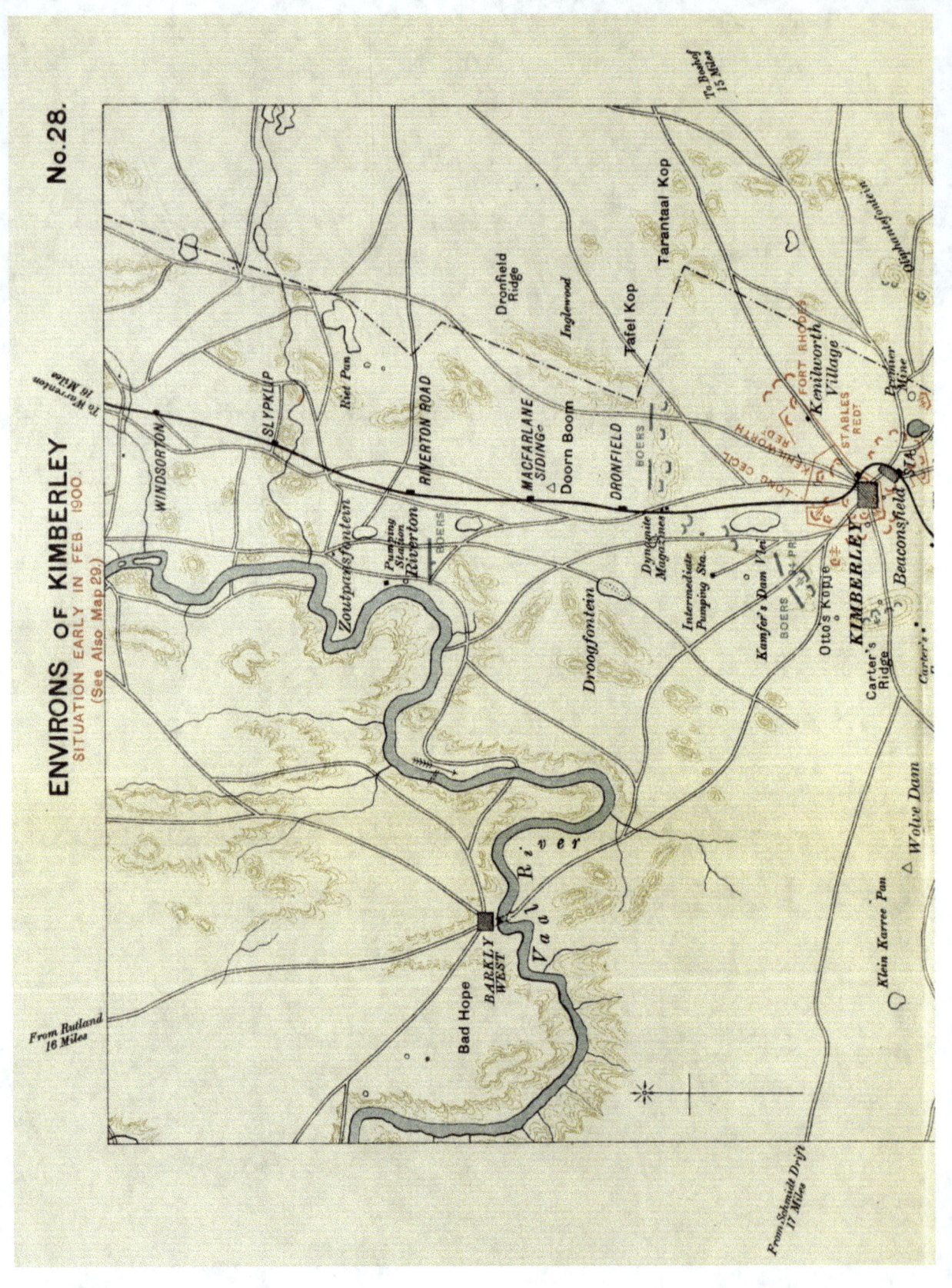

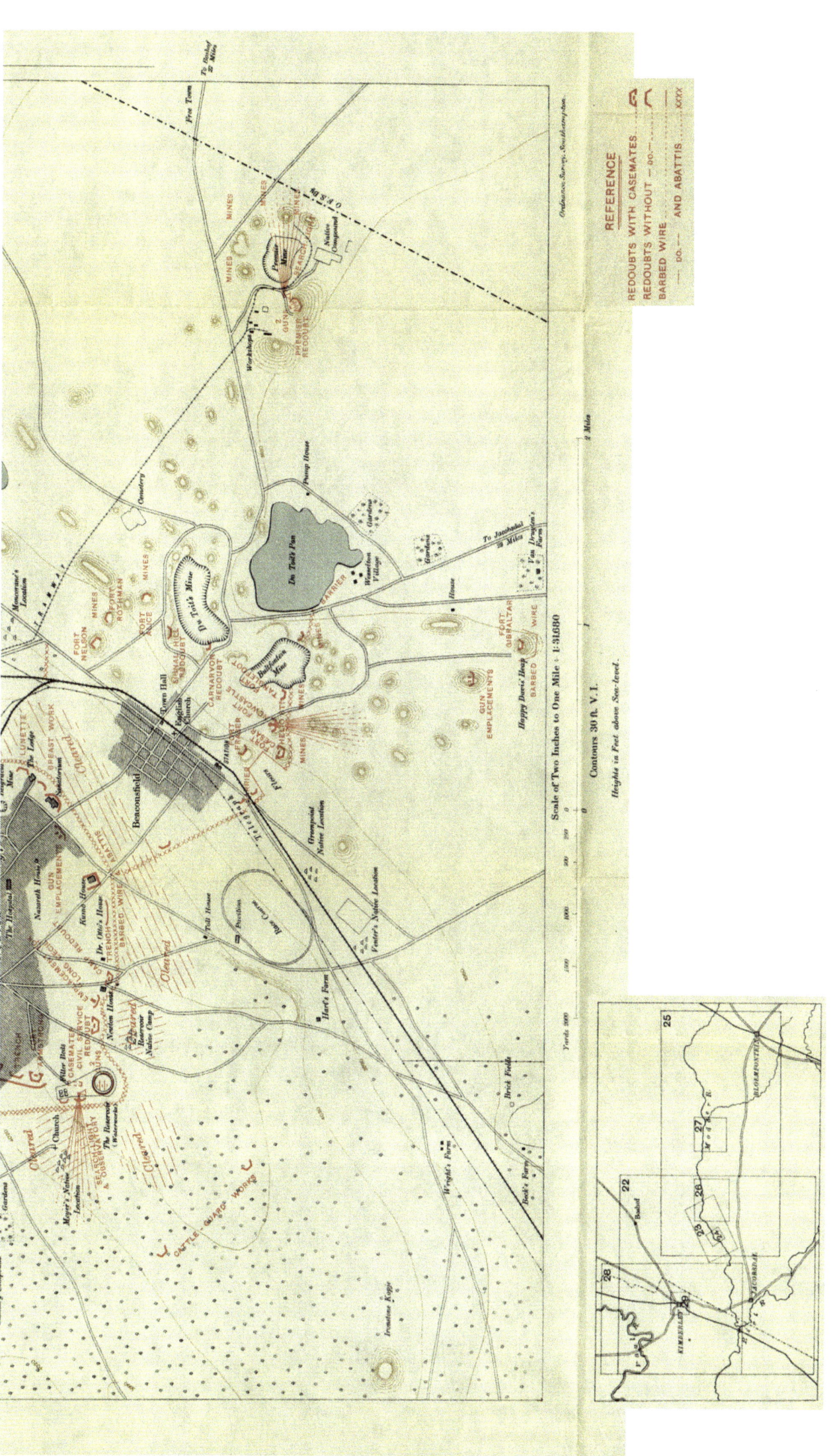

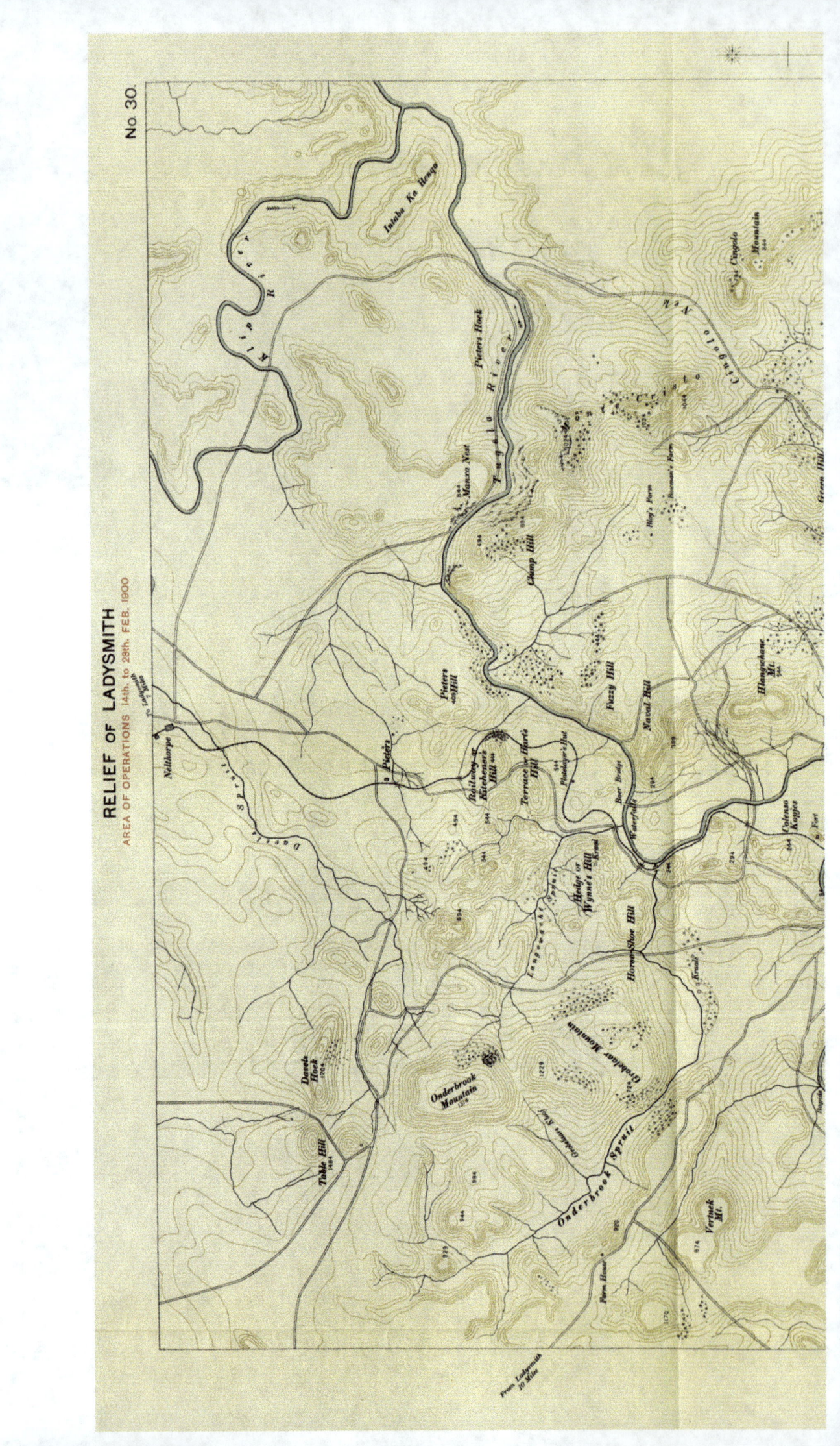

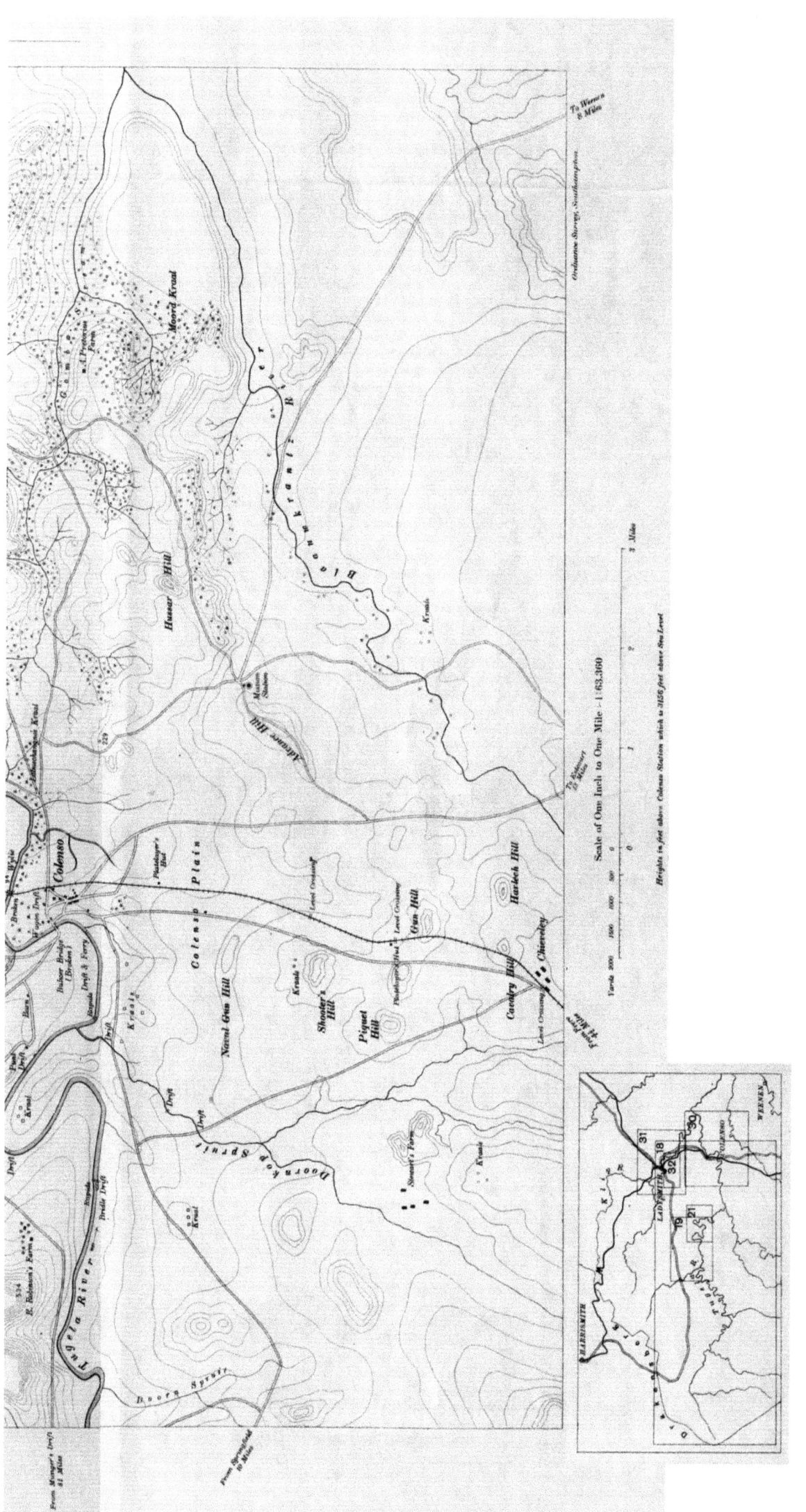

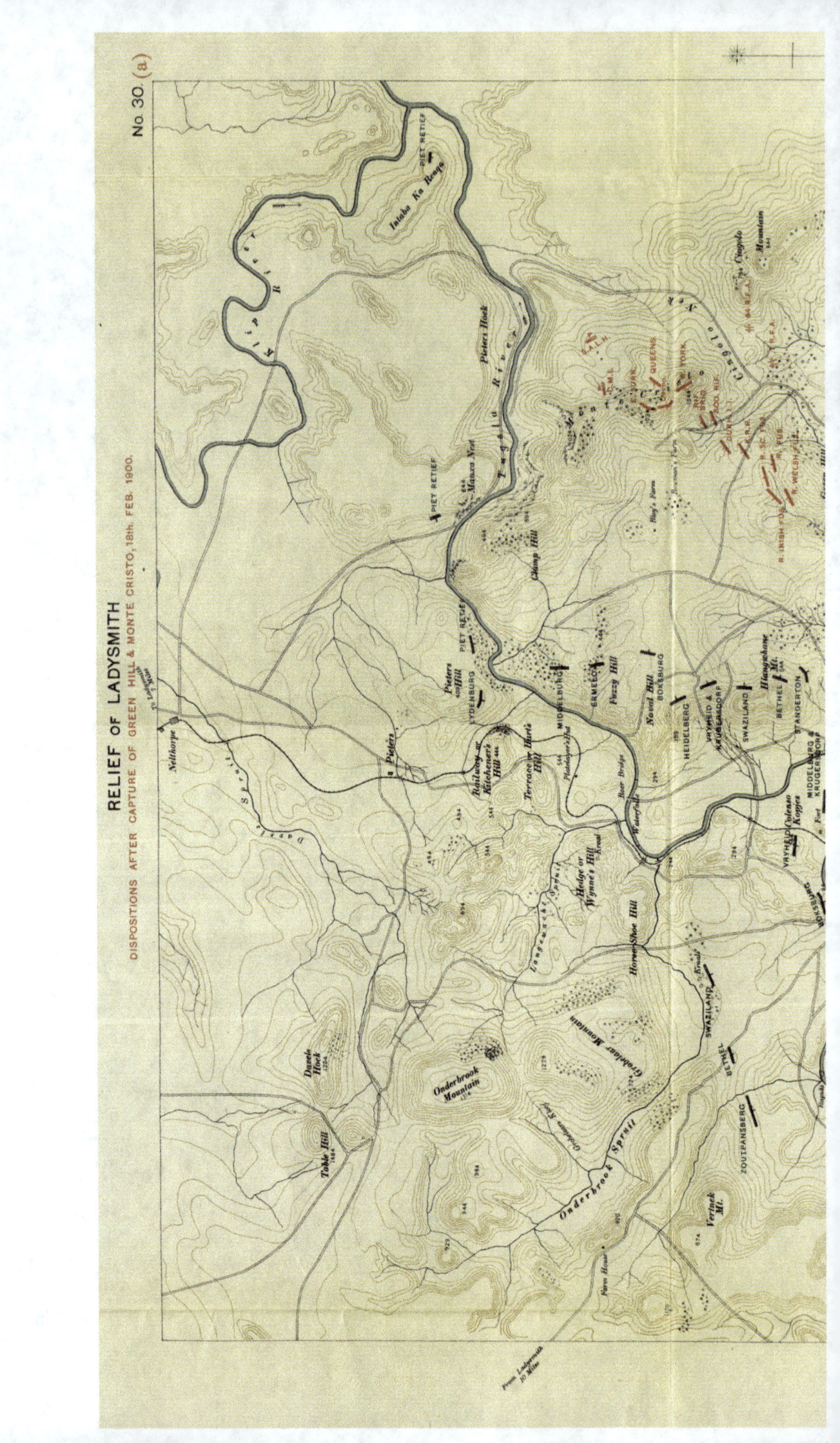

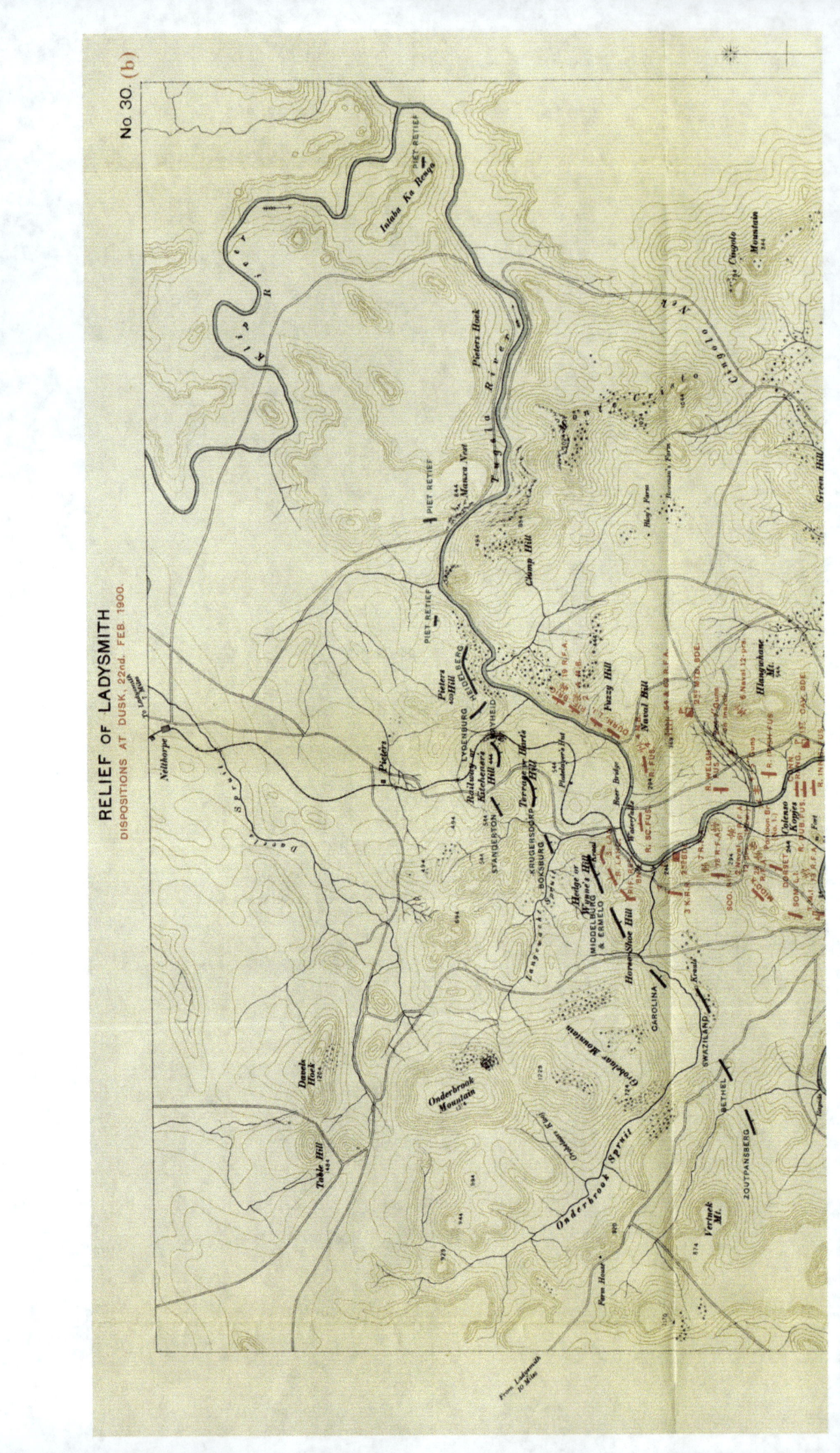

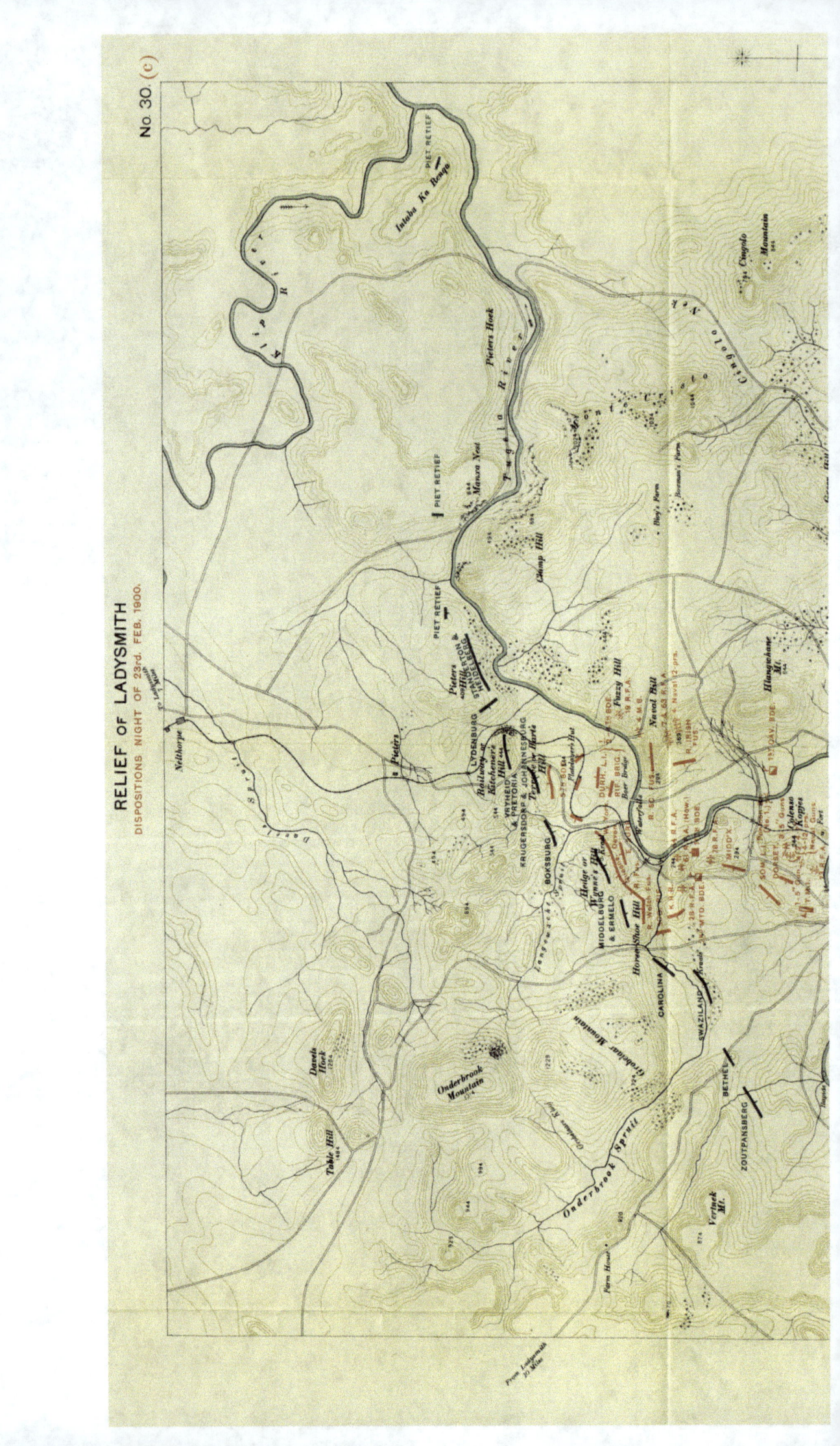

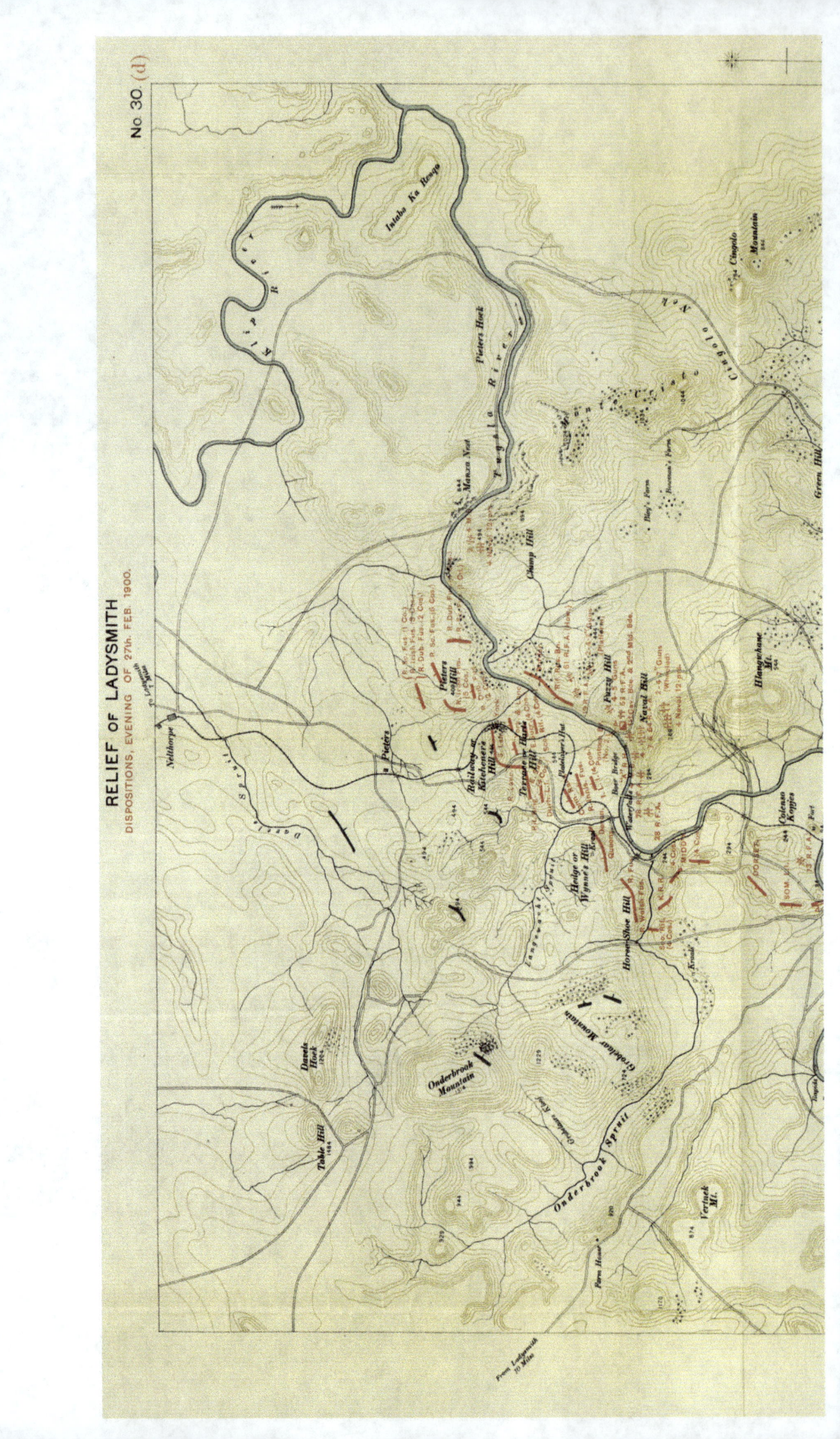

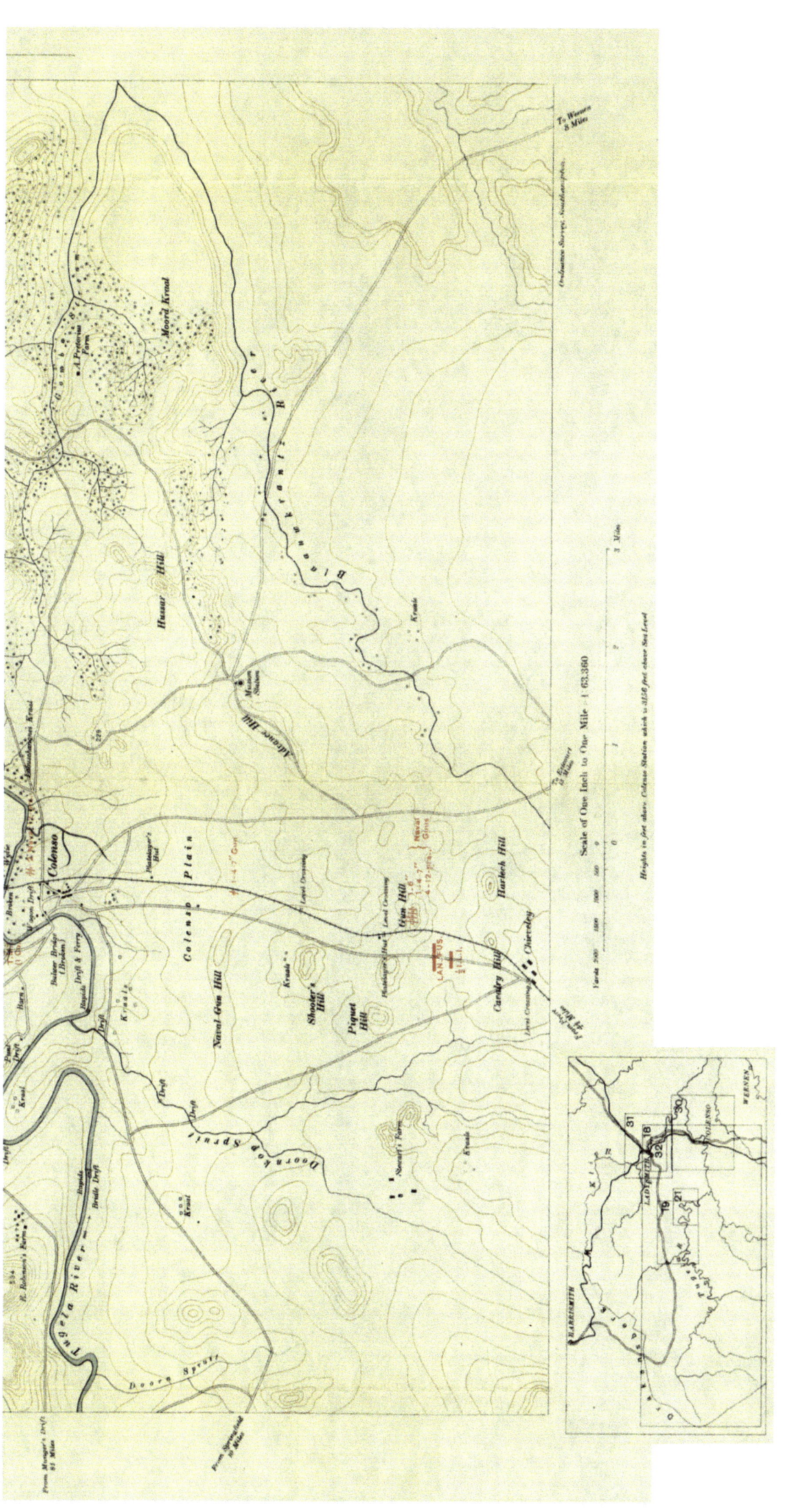

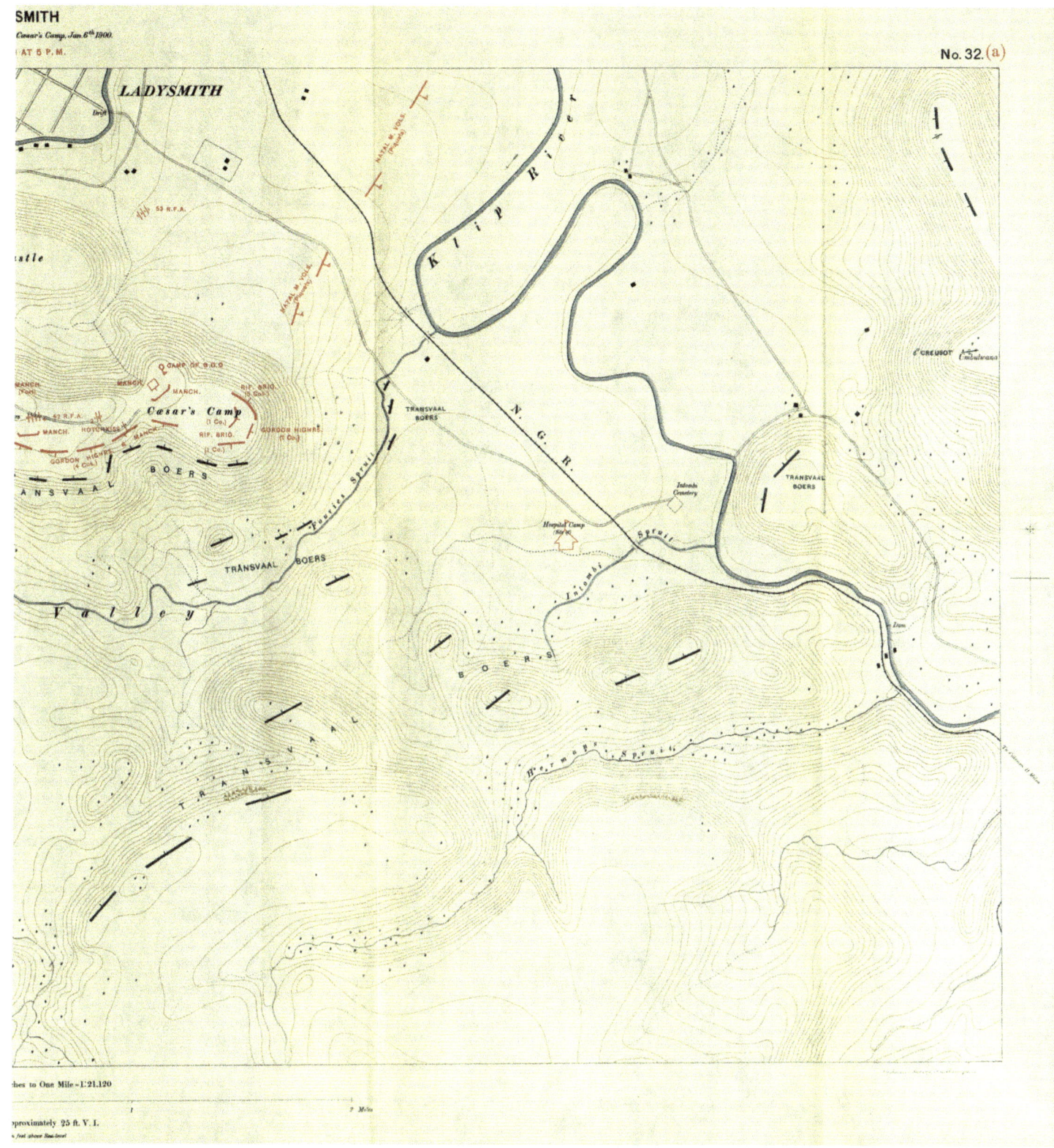

SITUATION
Krantzkraal
Mazelspoort
Roodraal
Brakleegte
Boesman's Kop
Grootpan
Waterval
Bathurst
Matjes Spruit
De Tank
Boesman's Kop
MARTYR'S
M.I.
Wagon Drift
Klein Groentepleats
Goedgenoeg
Doorn Hoek
Westpunt
Juistzoo
BOESMAN'S KOP OR VERCOE SIDING
Klein Klipkraal
From Bloemfontein 11½ Miles
Springfield
From Bloemfontein 10 Miles
Mealiespruit
Tusschenvier
Klein Palmietfontein
Potsdam
Waaikraal
Yards 2000 1500 1000 500 0
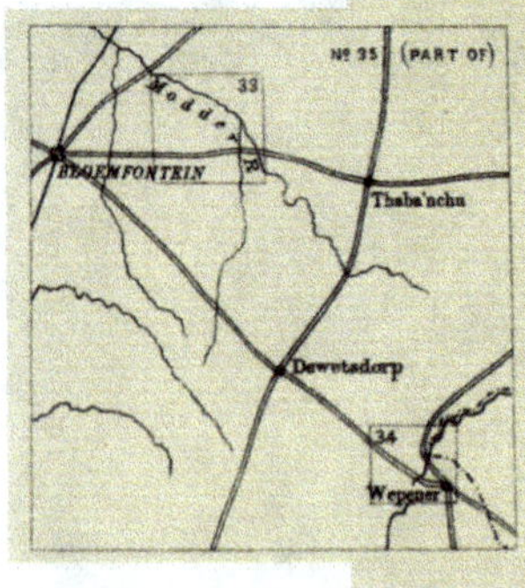
Nº 35 (PART OF)
33
Modder R.
Thaba'nchu
Dewetsdorp
34
Wepener

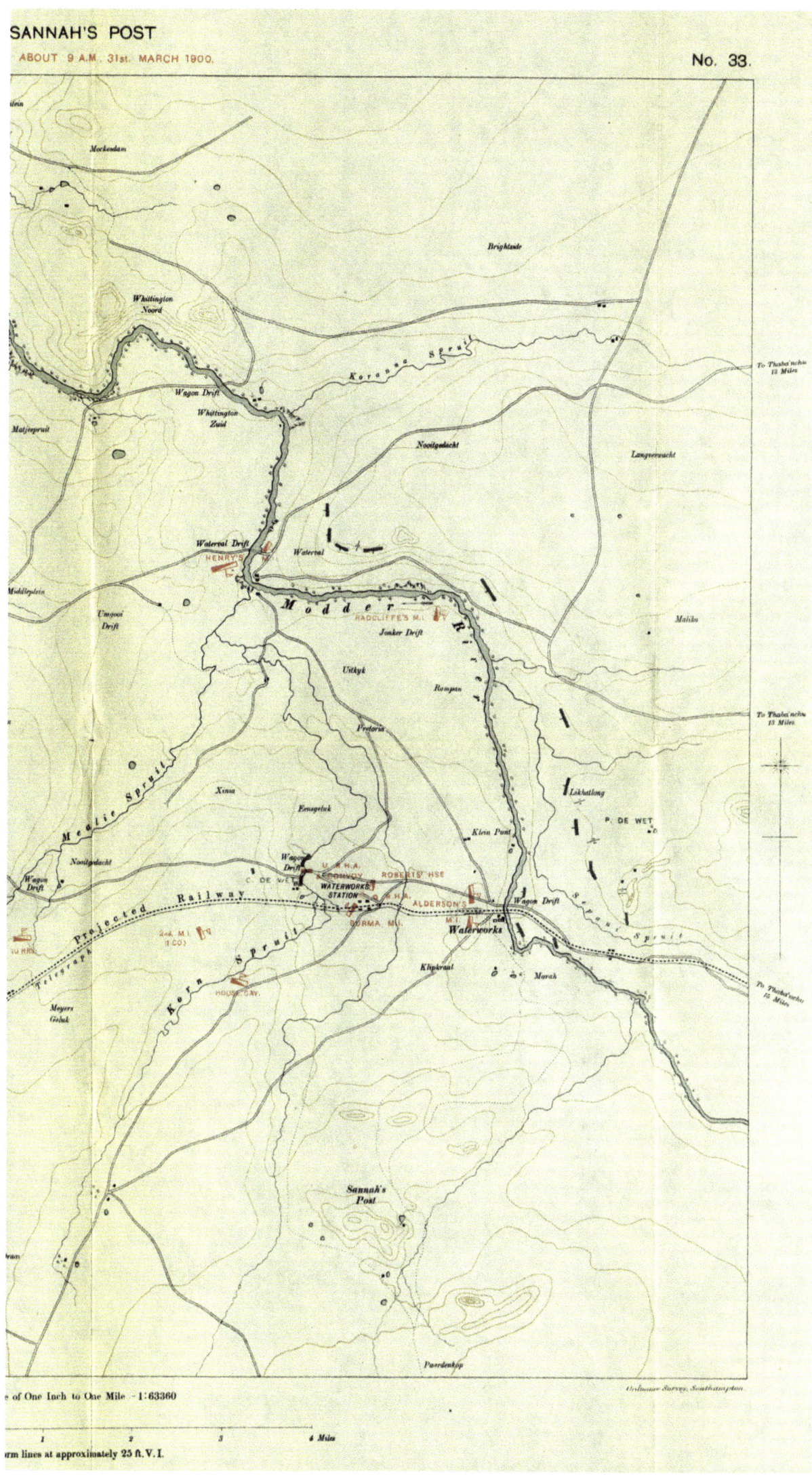

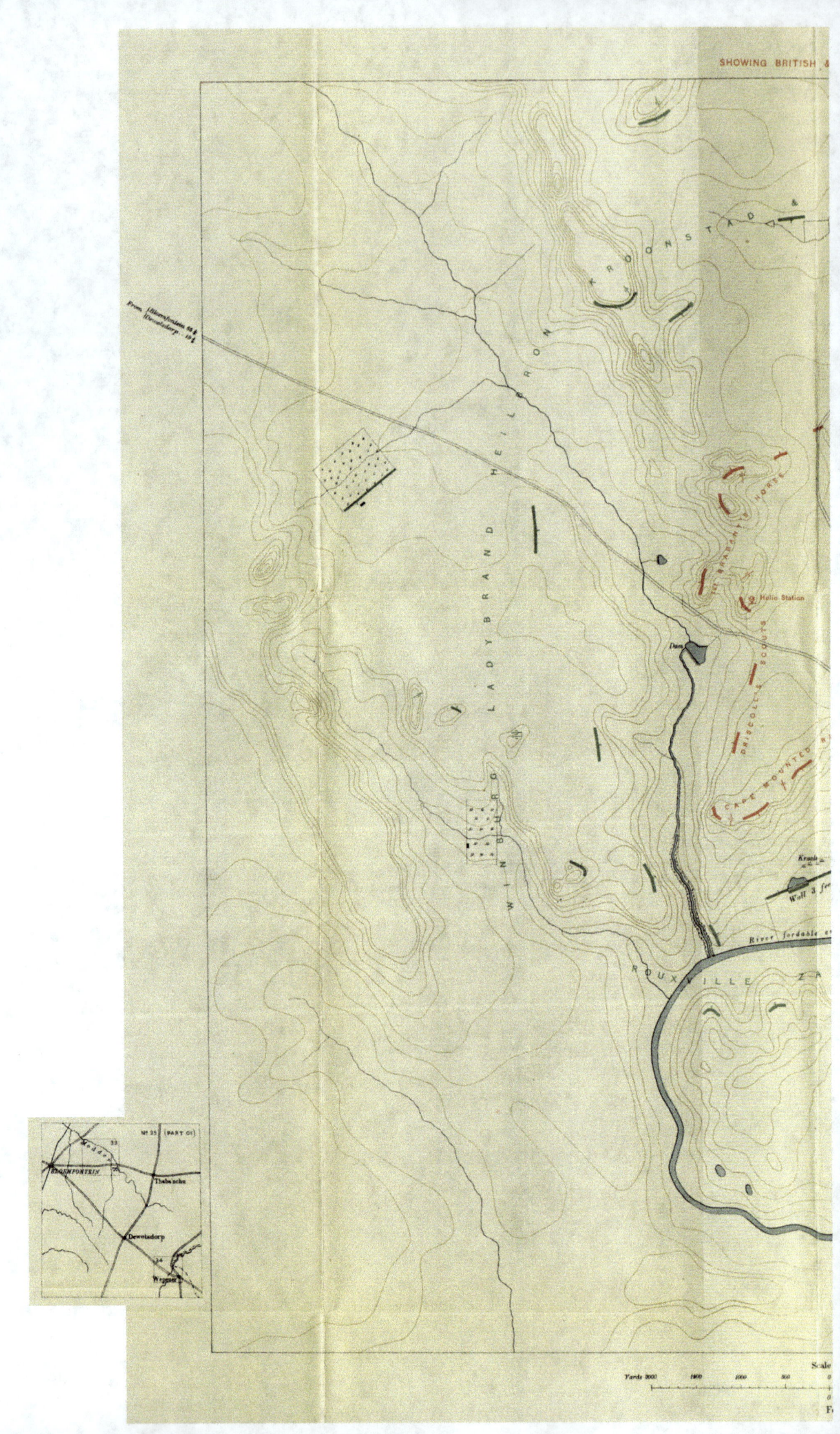

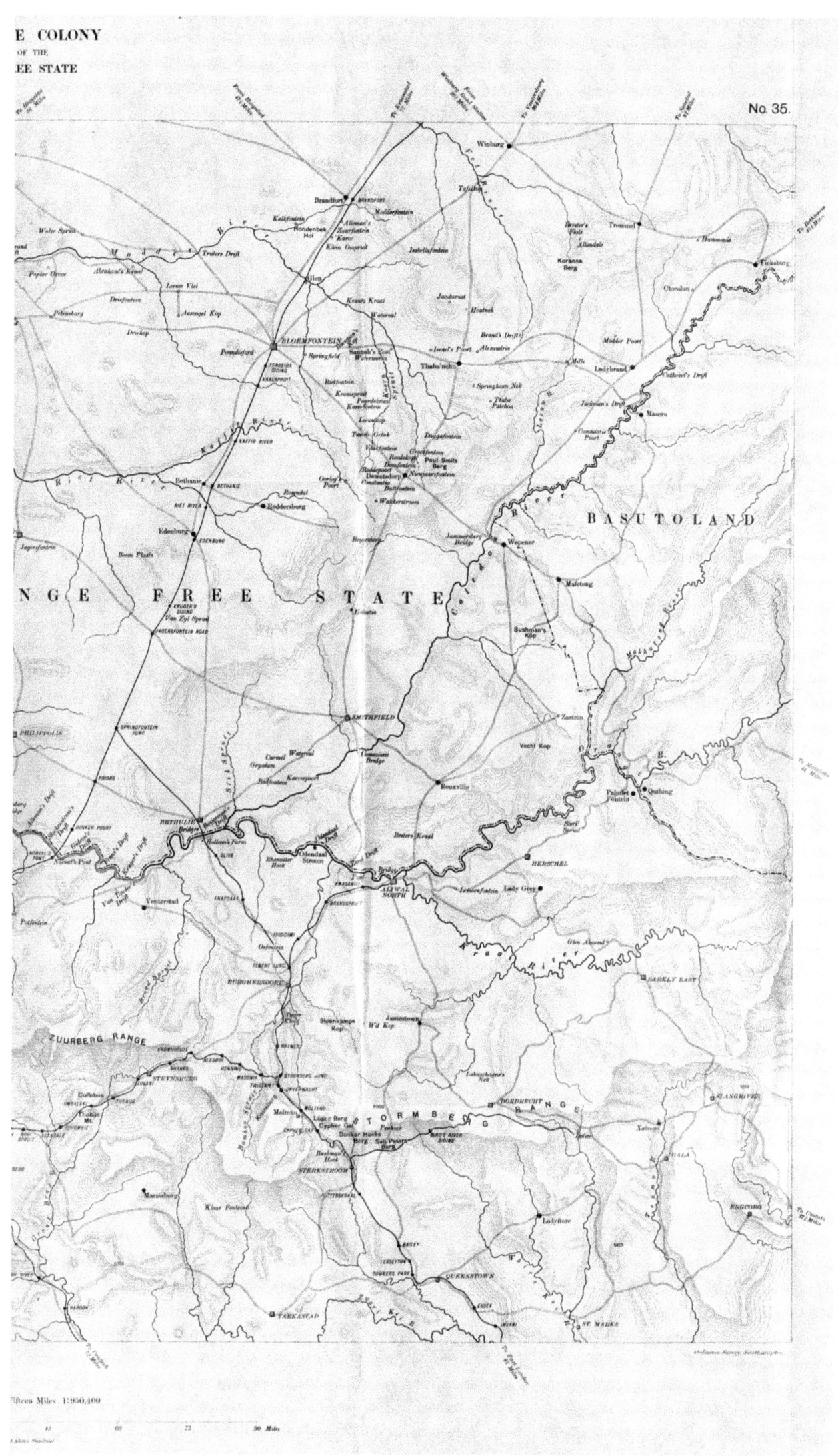

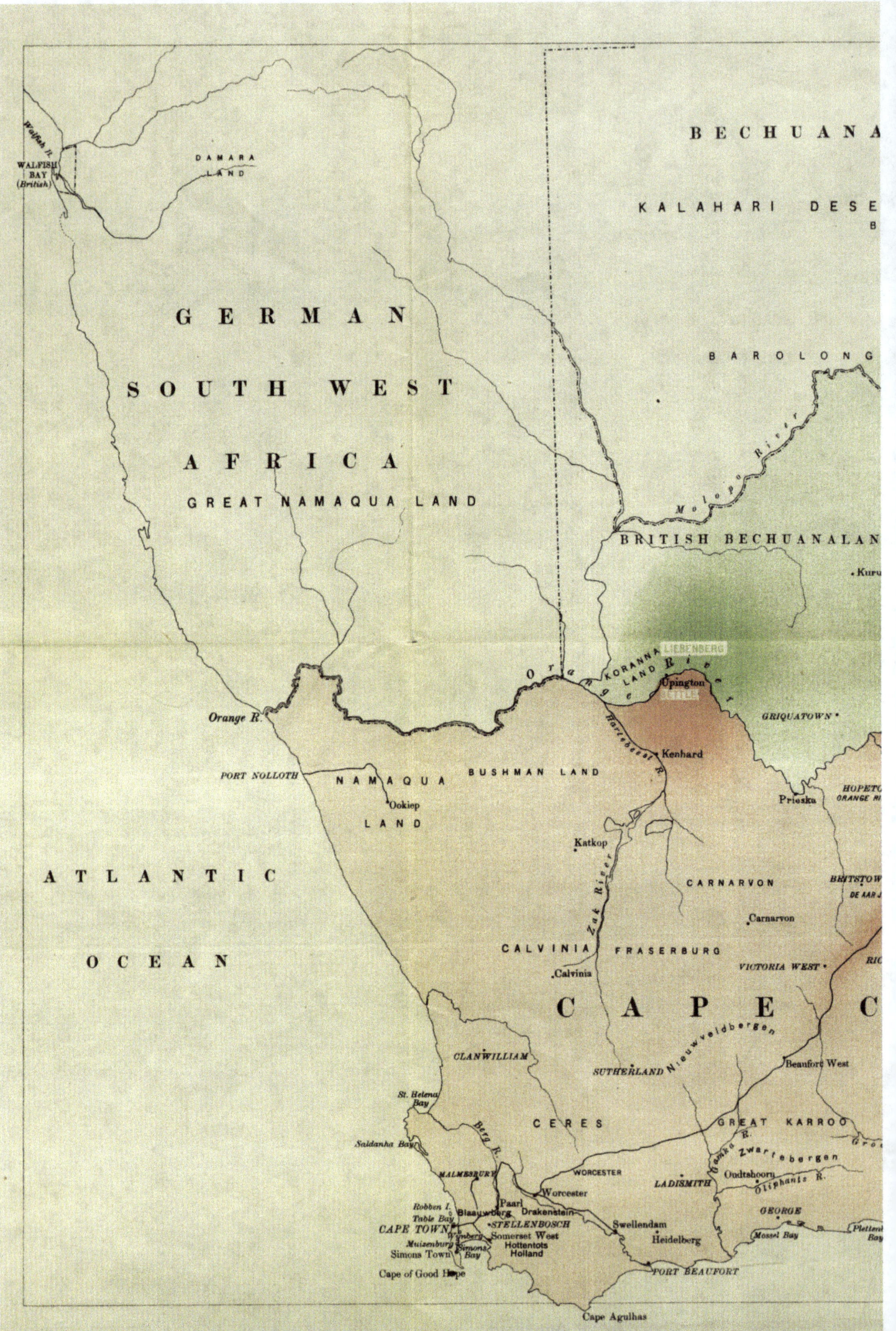

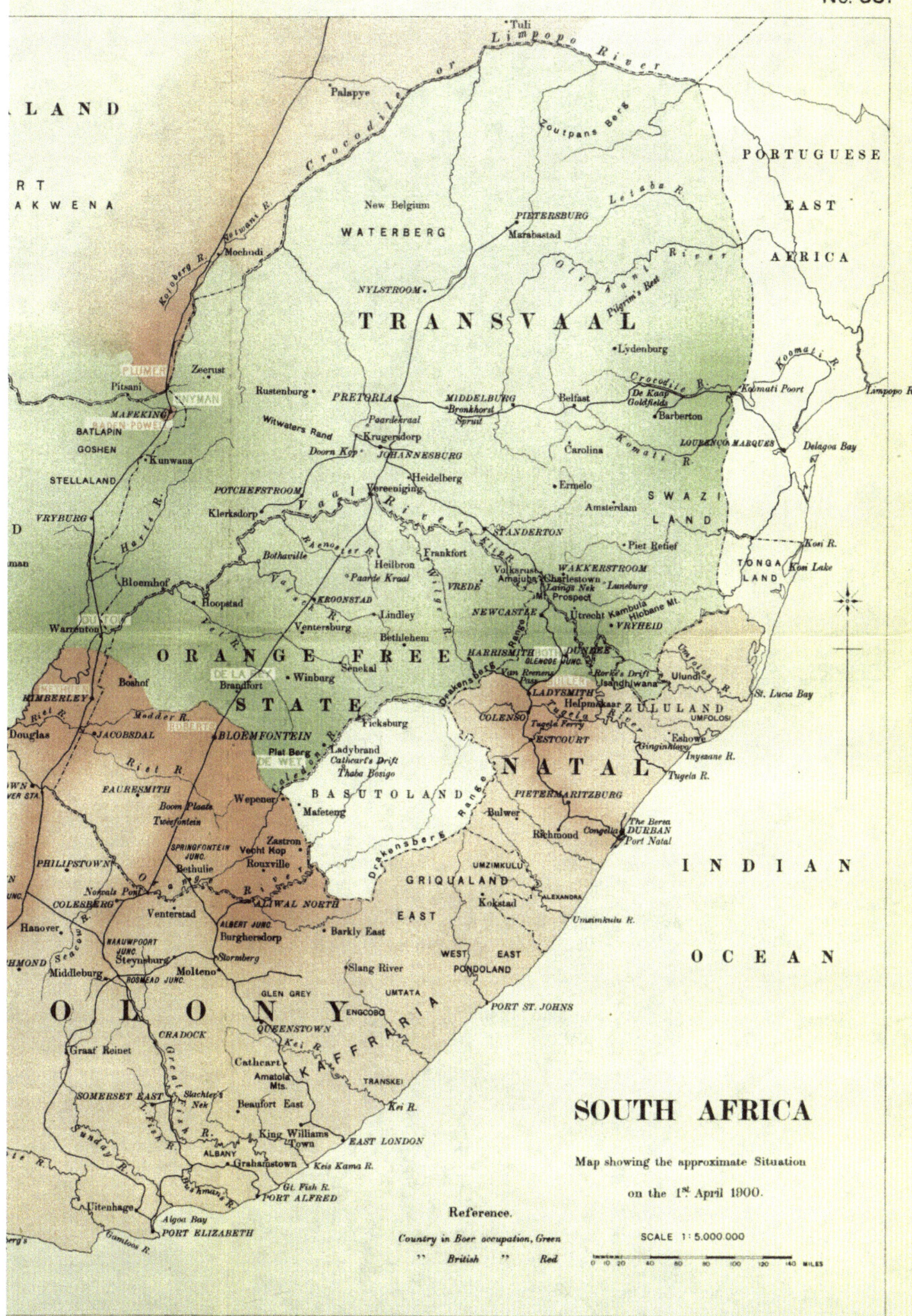

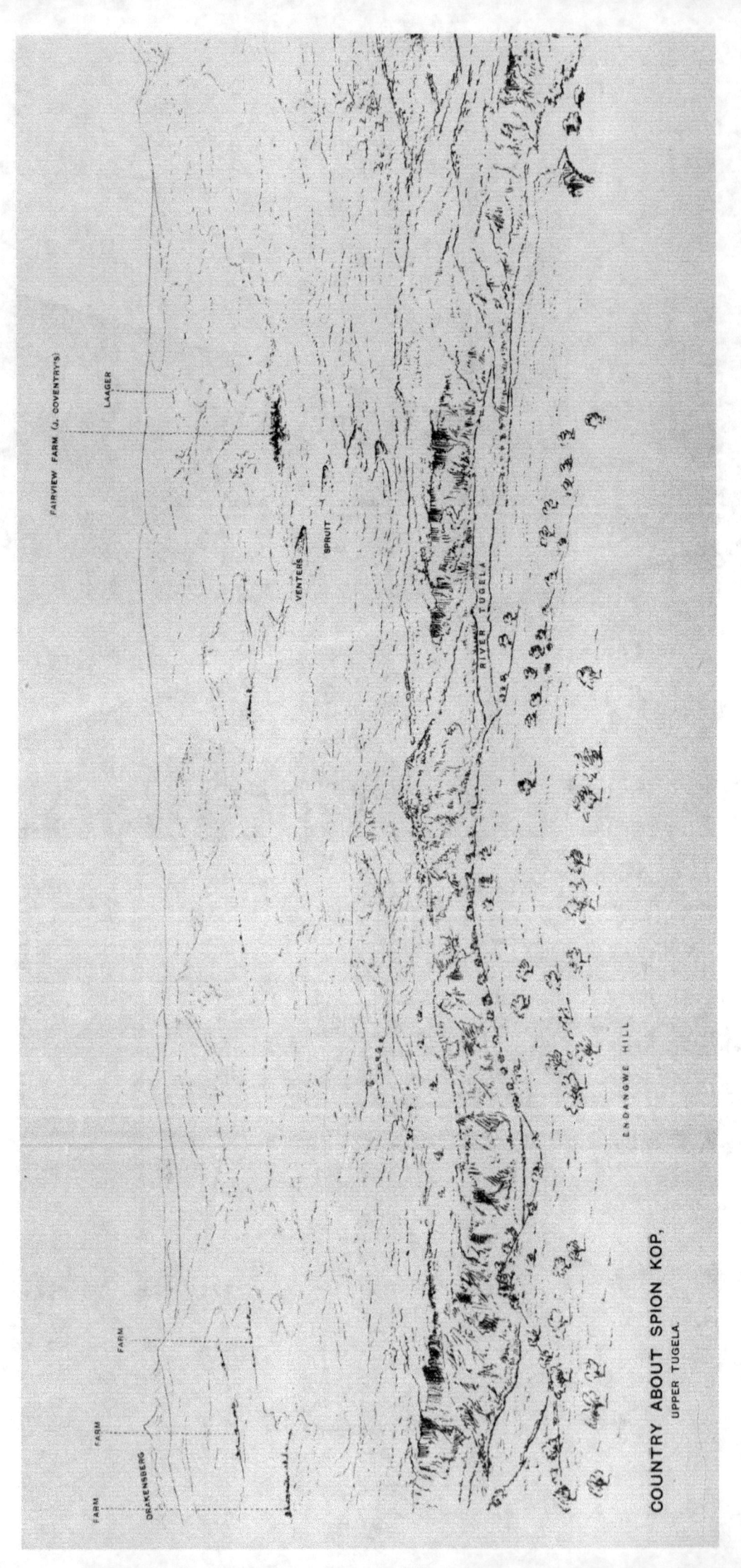

COUNTRY ABOUT SPION KOP,
UPPER TUGELA.

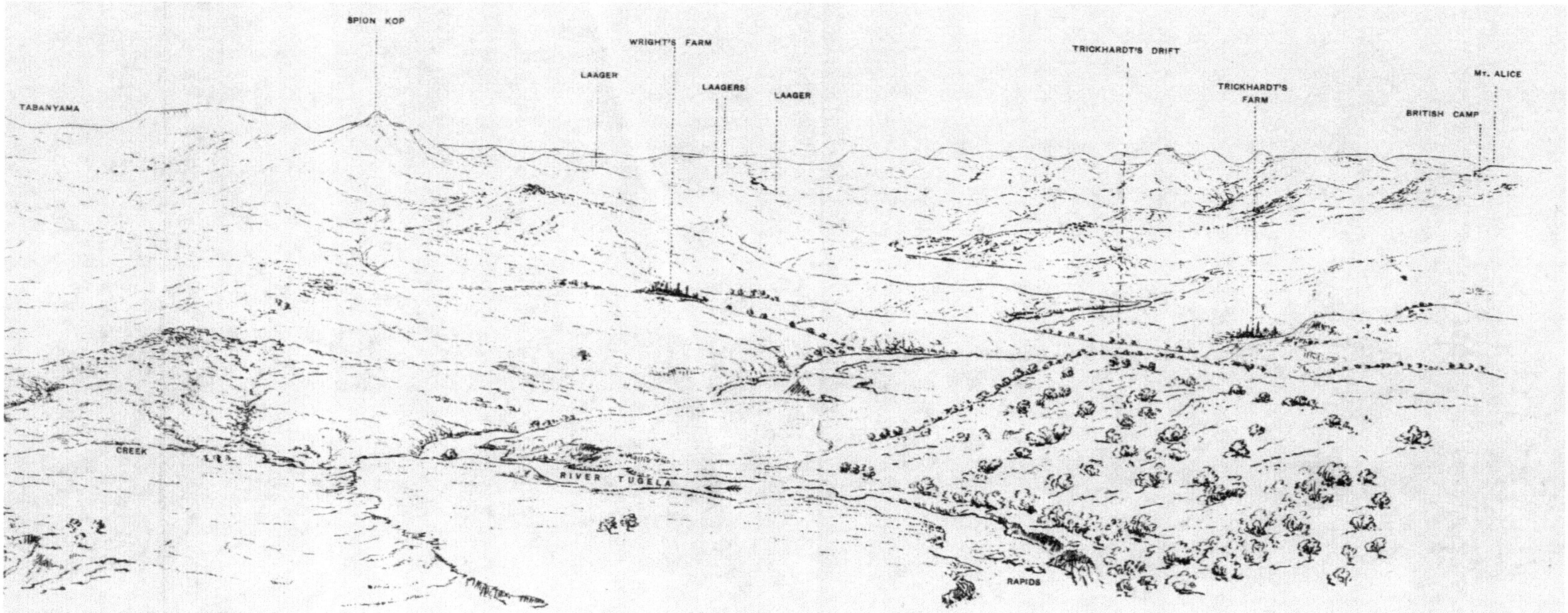

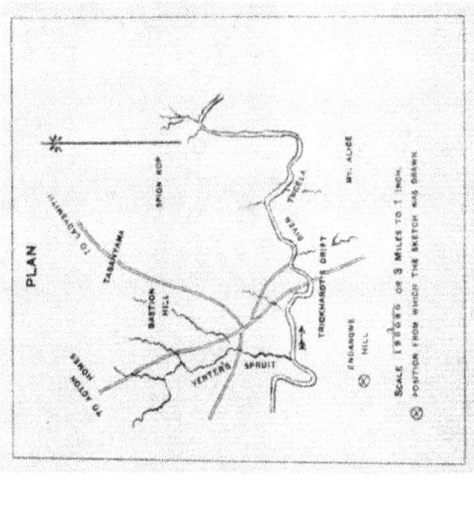

COUNTRY ABOUT SPION KOP LOOKING N.E. FROM ENDANGWE HILL,
FROM AN UNFINISHED DRAWING DATED 73-1-00 BY THE LATE CAPTAIN W. C. EPRICHE, R.B.I.
COMPLETED BY CAPTAIN K. W. DAVIE, GLOUCESTER REGIMENT.

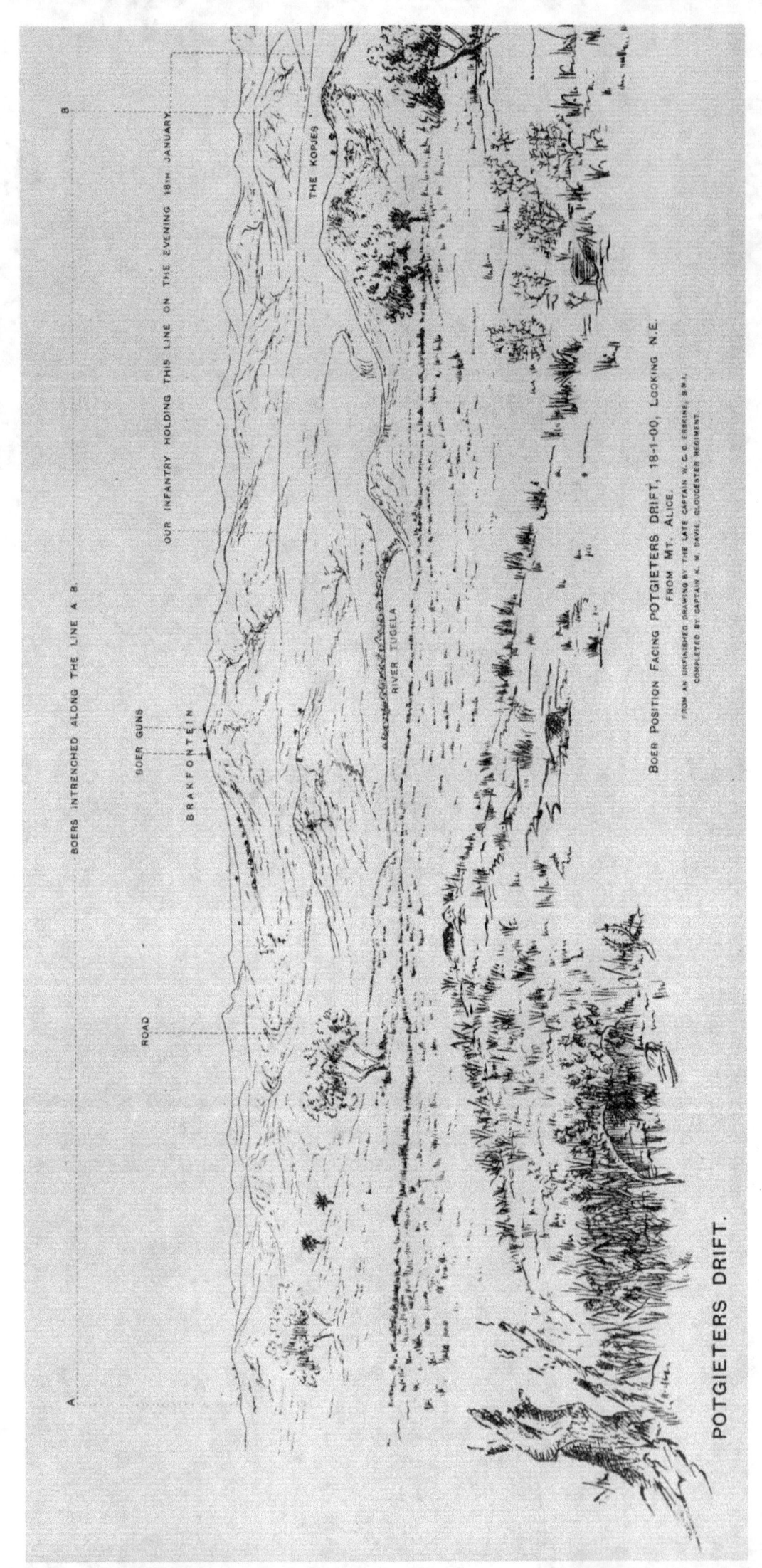

POTGIETERS DRIFT.

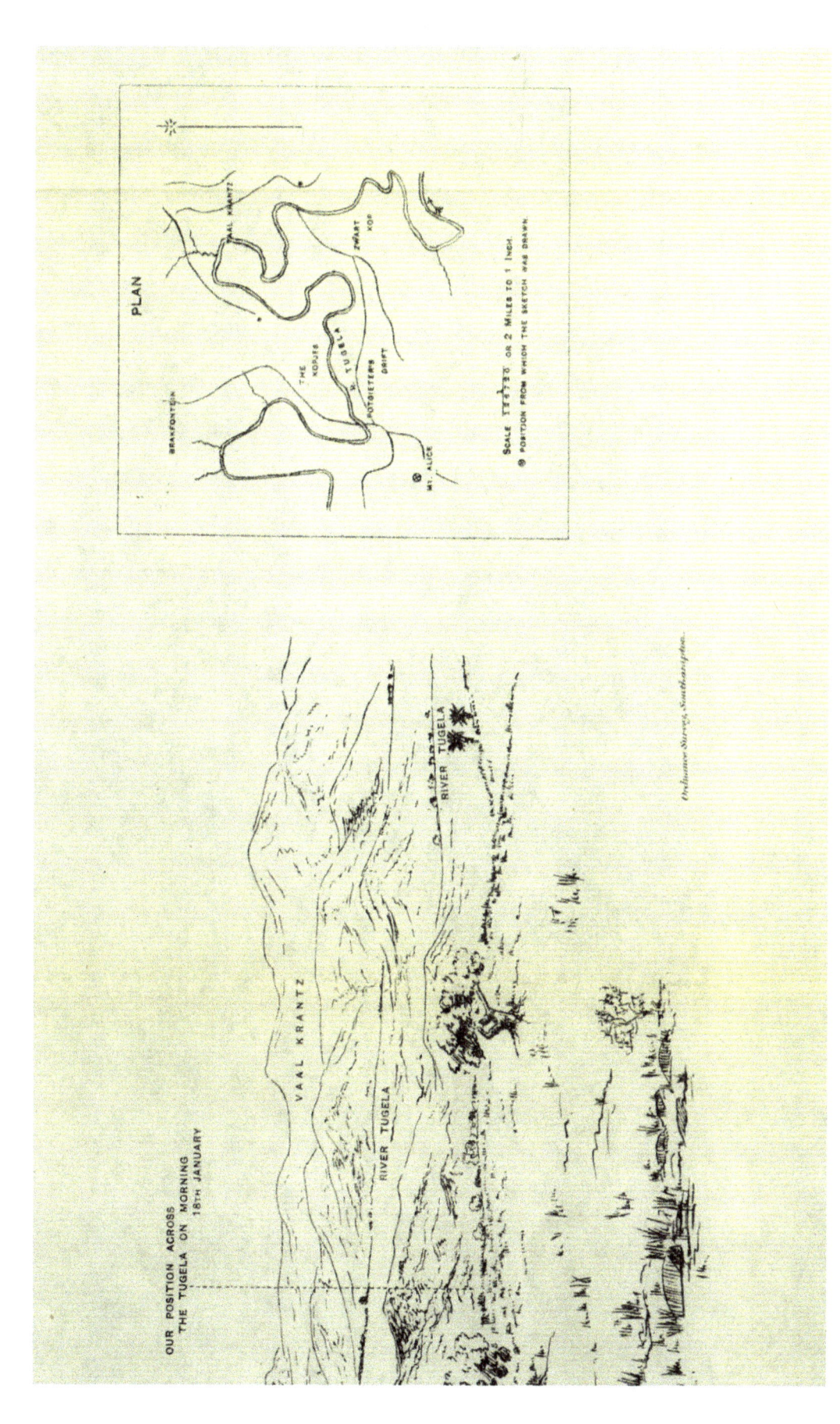

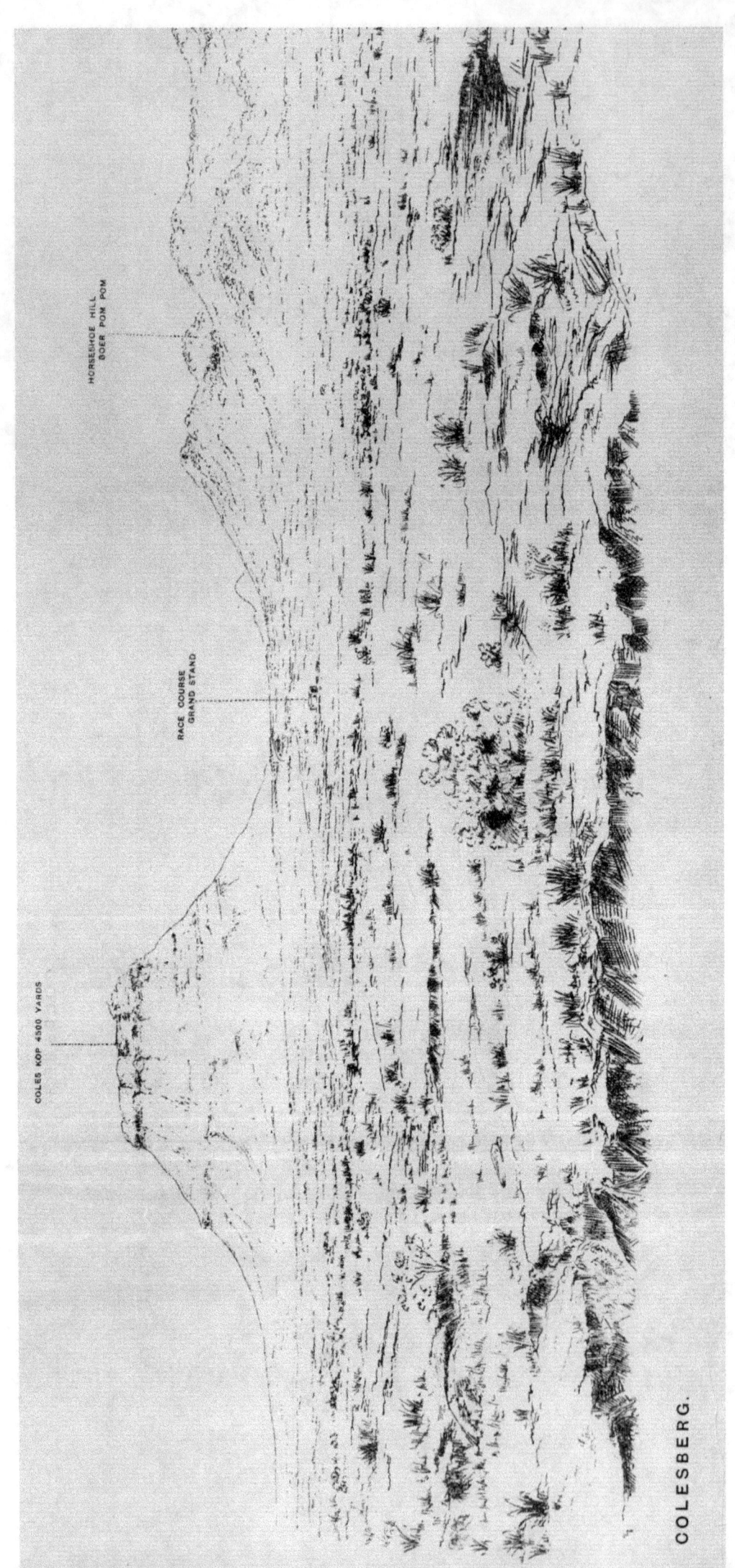

COLESBERG.

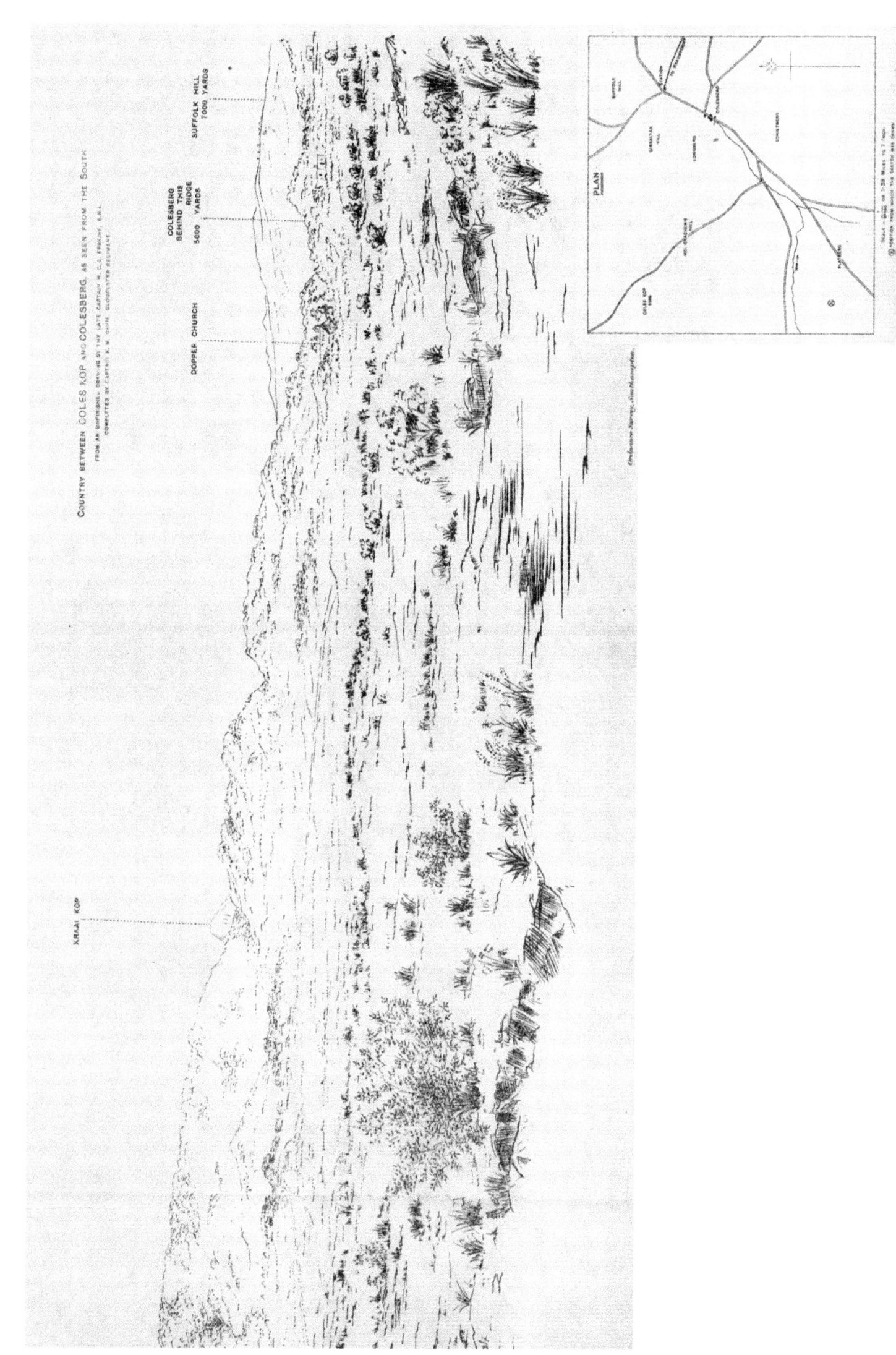

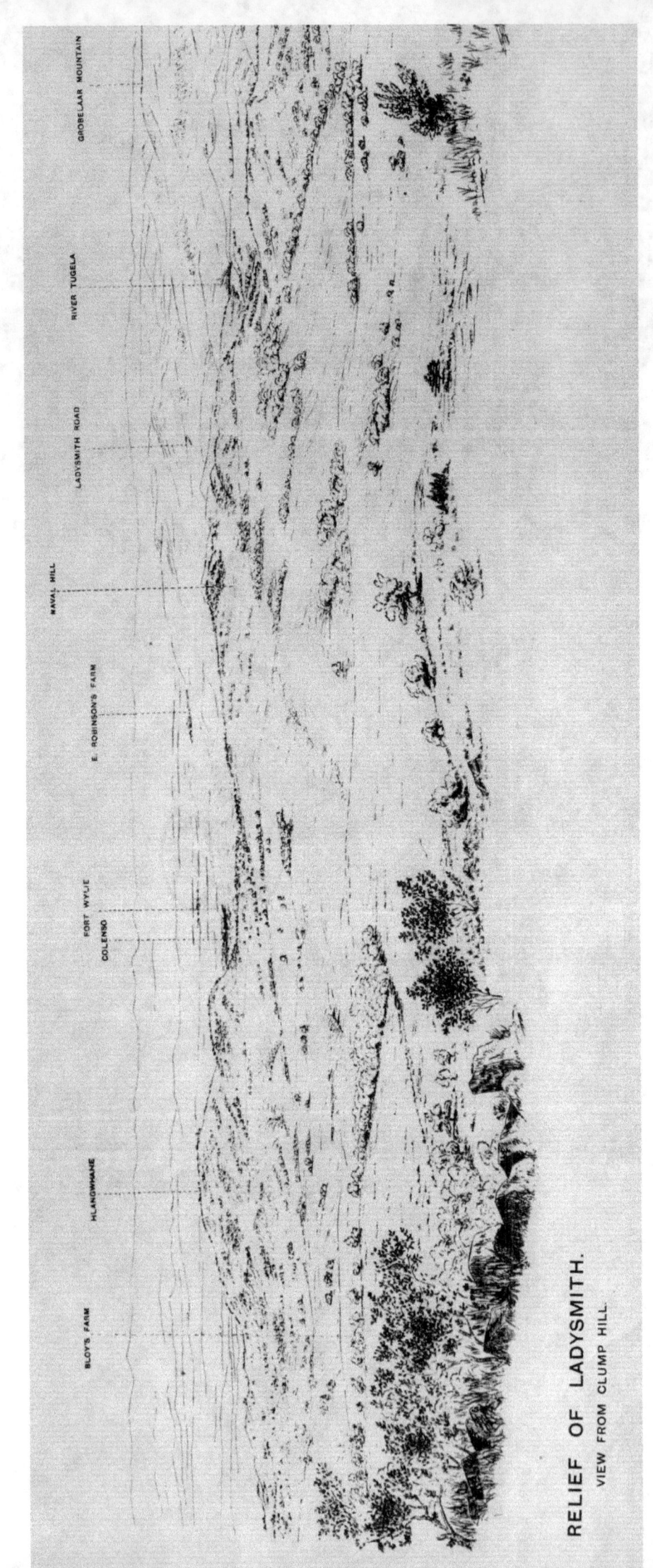

TERRACE OR HART'S HILL
ONDERBROOK MOUNTAIN
RAILWAY OR KITCHENER'S HILL
PIETER'S HILL S. KOPJE
RIVER TUGELA
PIETER'S HILL N. KOPJE
PIETER'S STATION
Ordnance Survey, Southampton.

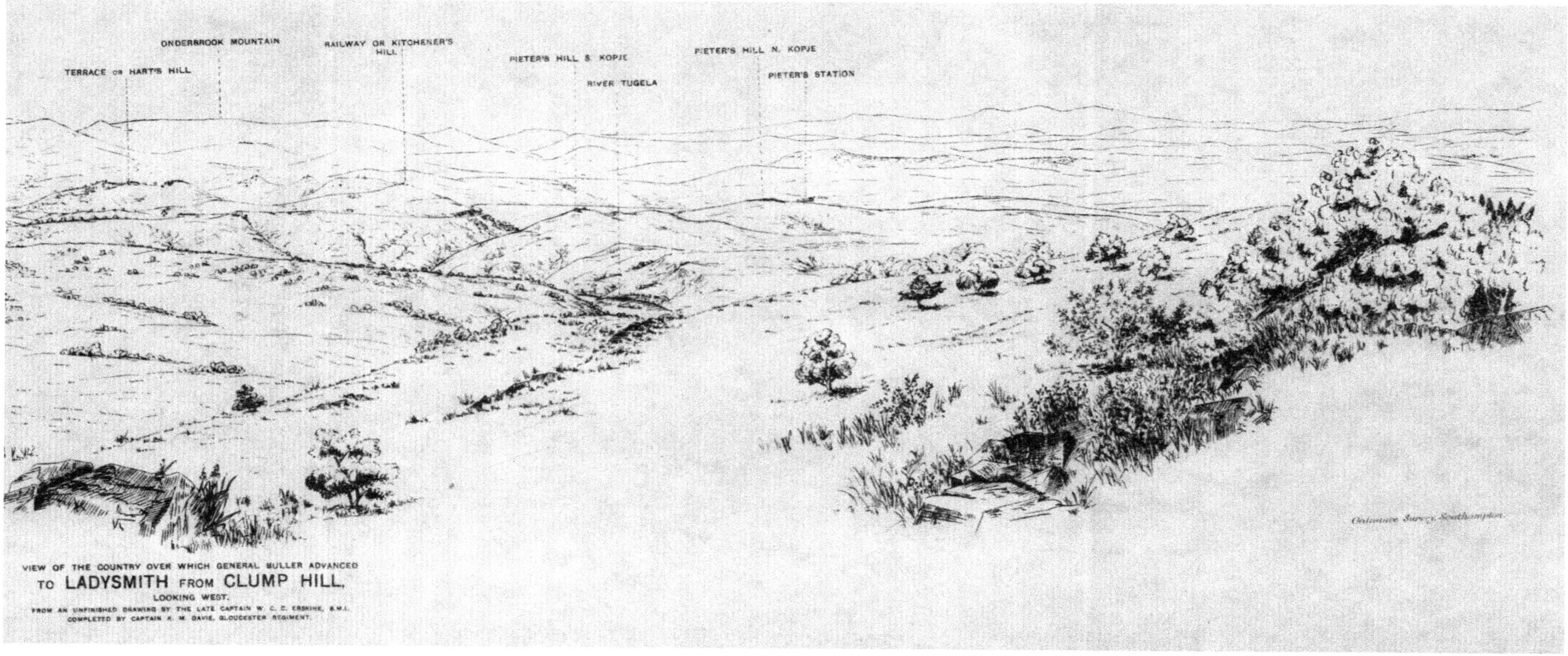

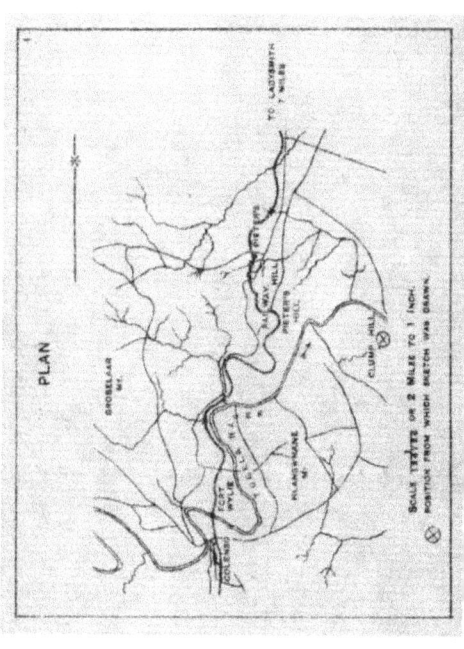

VIEW OF THE COUNTRY OVER WHICH GENERAL BULLER ADVANCED
TO LADYSMITH FROM CLUMP HILL,
LOOKING WEST.
FROM AN UNFINISHED DRAWING BY THE LATE CAPTAIN W. C. C. ERSKINE, R.M.I.
COMPLETED BY CAPTAIN H. M. DAVIE, GLOUCESTER REGIMENT.

PLAN
GROBELAAR MT.
COLENSO
FORT WYLIE
TUGELA R.
HLANGWHANE M.
RAILWAY HILL
PIETER'S
PIETER'S HILL
CLUMP HILL
TO LADYSMITH 7 MILES
POSITION FROM WHICH SKETCH WAS DRAWN.

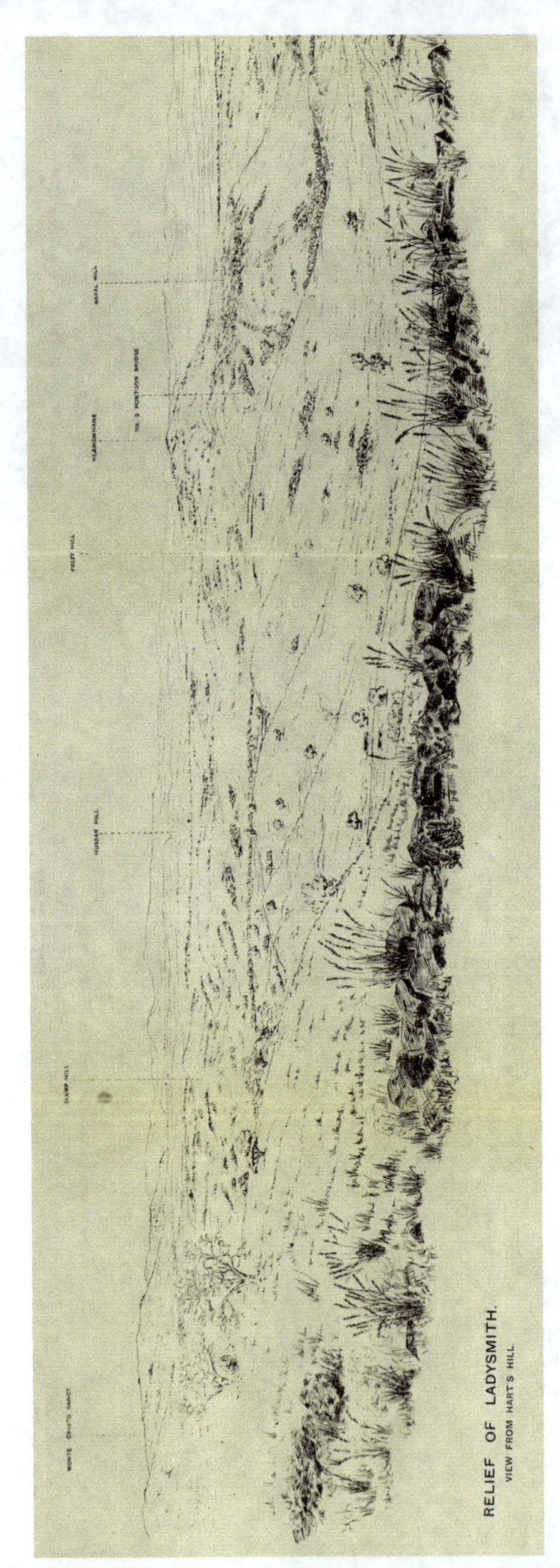

RELIEF OF LADYSMITH.
VIEW FROM HART'S HILL.

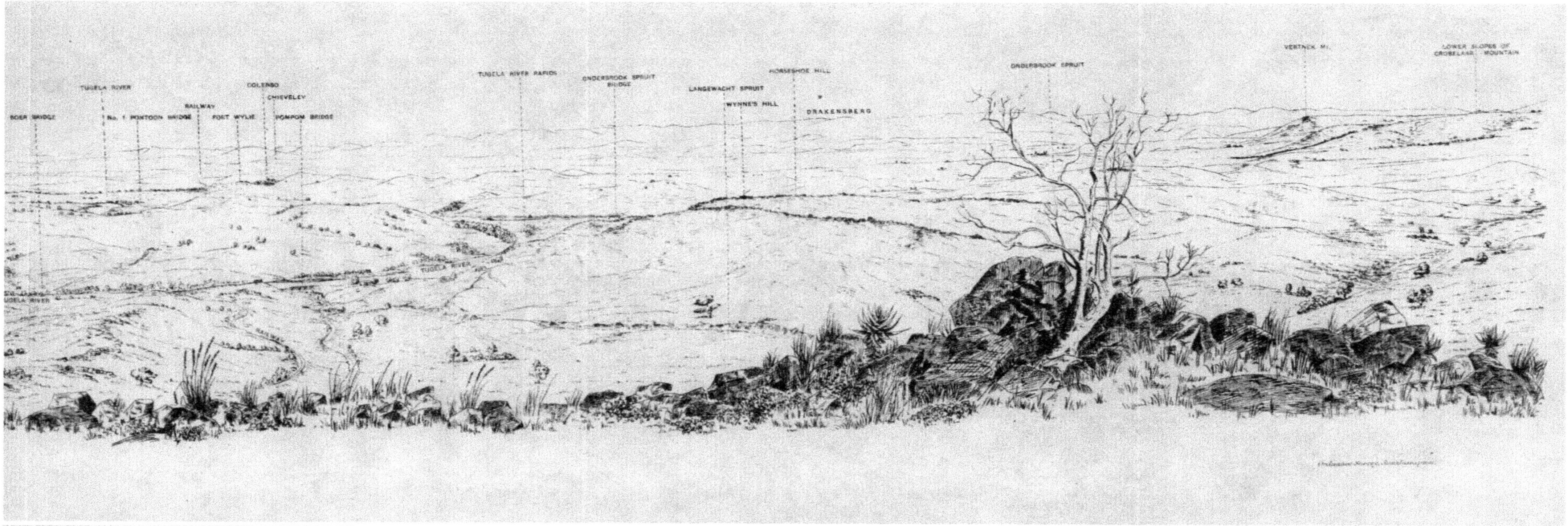

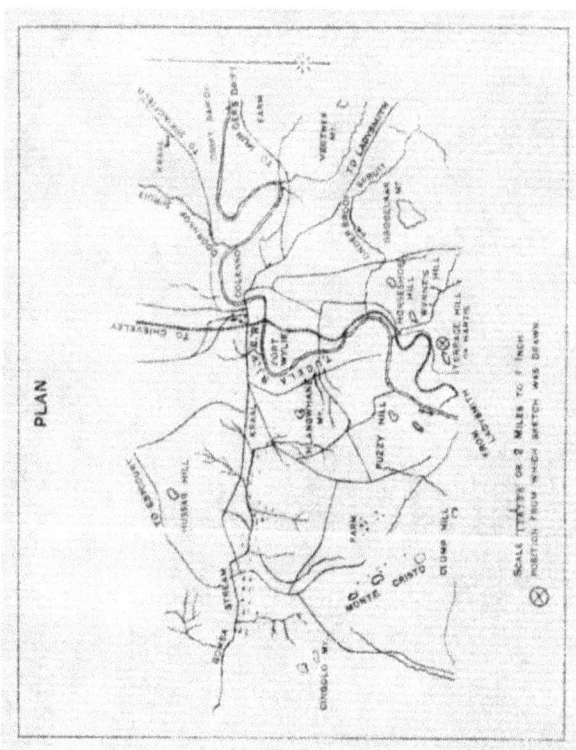

PART OF THE COUNTRY OVER WHICH SIR R. BULLER ADVANCED TO THE
RELIEF OF LADYSMITH.

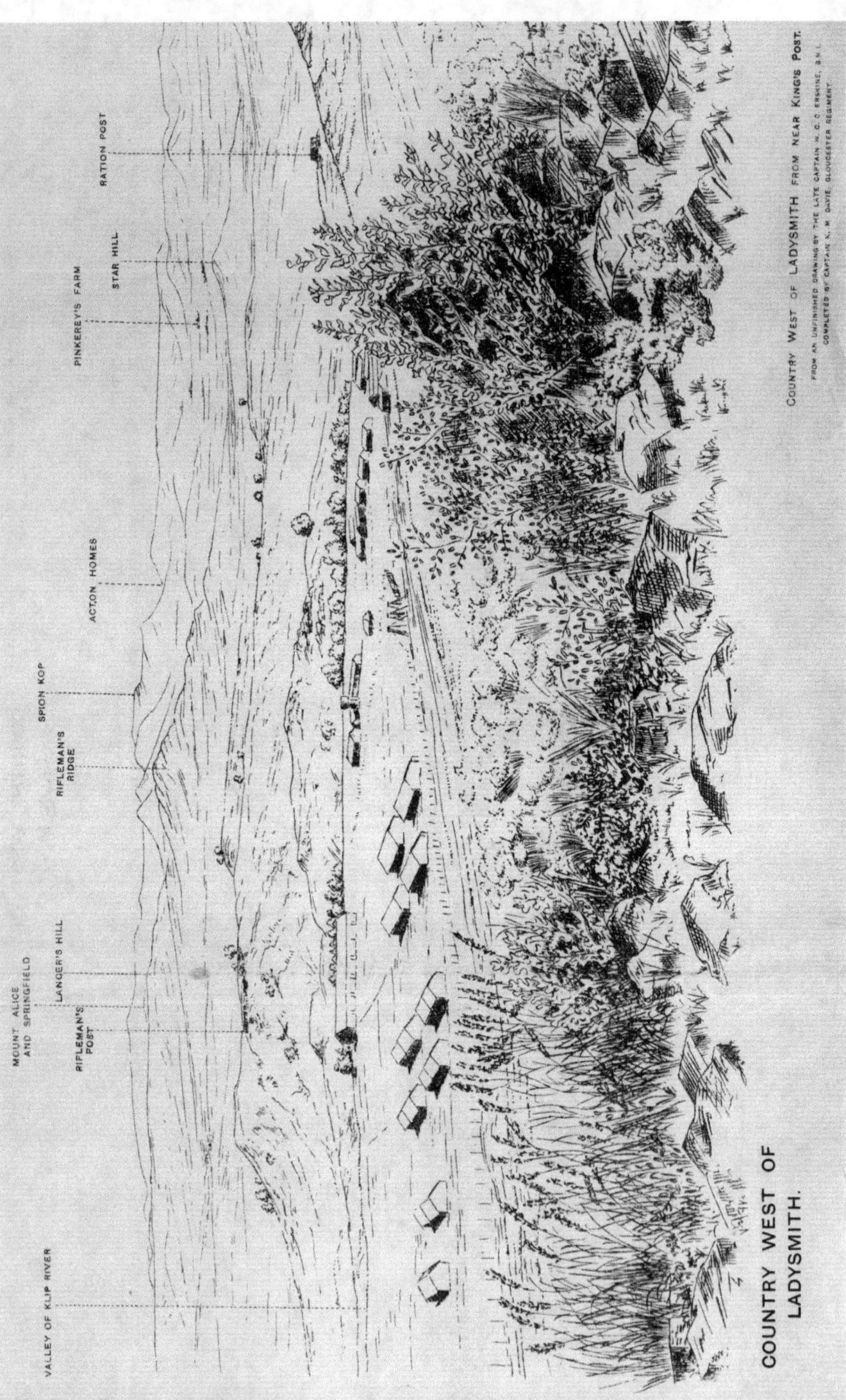

COUNTRY WEST OF LADYSMITH FROM NEAR KING'S POST.

From an unfinished drawing by the late Captain W. C. Erskine, 3.L.I. Completed by Captain K. M. Davie, Gloucester Regiment.

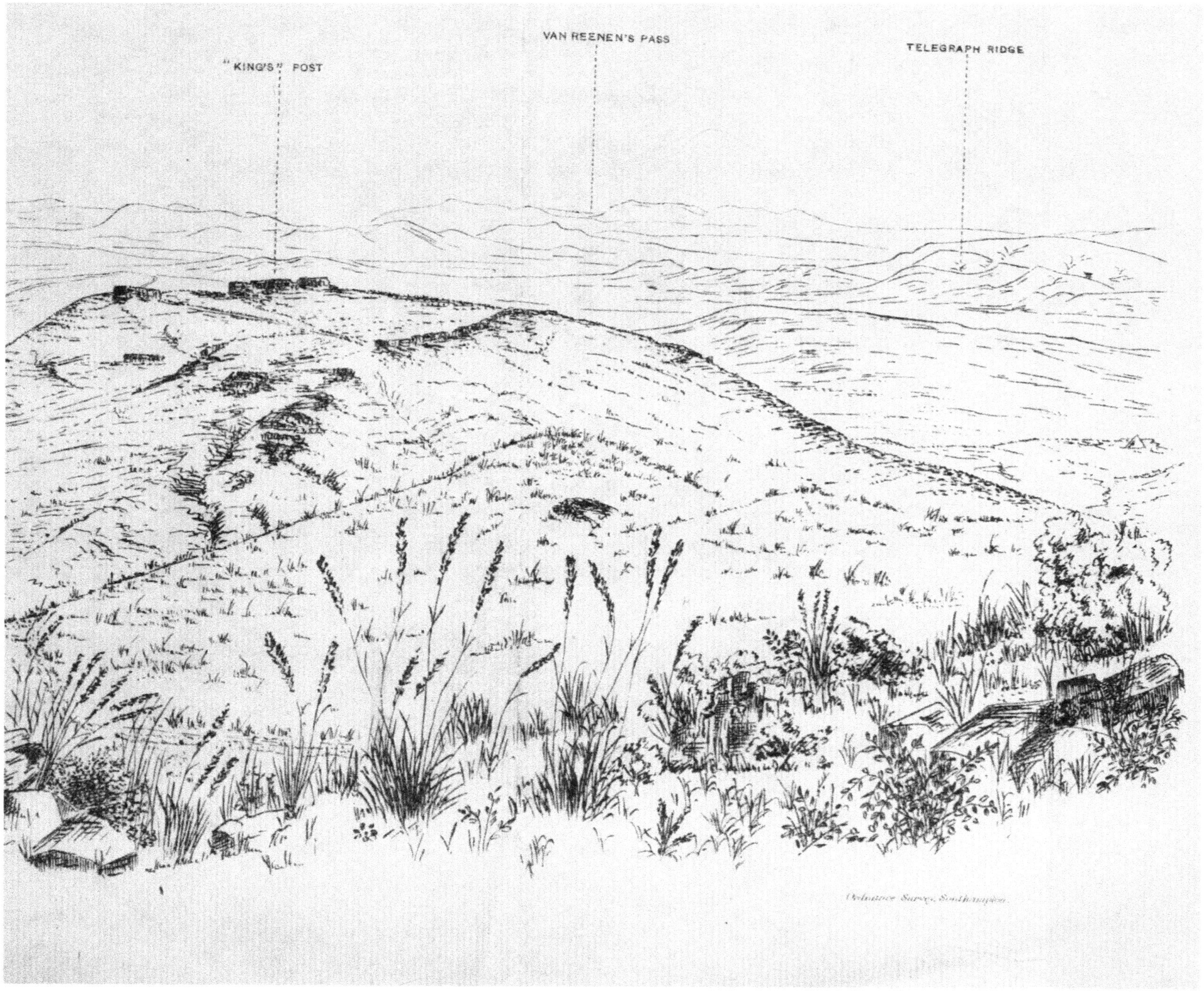
"KING'S" POST
VAN REENEN'S PASS
TELEGRAPH RIDGE
Ordnance Survey, Southampton.

PLAN
TELEGRAPH RIDGE
STAR HILL
FROM COLENSO
13 MILES
RANGE POST
RATION POST
LEICESTER POST
OBSERVATION HILL
LADYSMITH

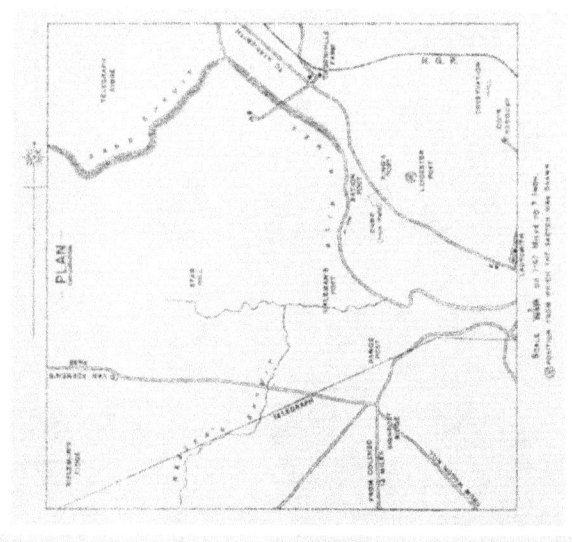

www.ingramcontent.com/pod-product-compliance
Lightning Source LLC
Chambersburg PA
CBHW080834010526
44112CB00016B/2511